Dirty Teacher

I had to get away.

In the week before leaving for Korea, I made a final trip to work. After purchasing a large Tim Horton's coffee, I drove down the Lougheed Highway, feeling the same grooves in the road I'd felt for forever.

Traffic at noon was always fairly light heading east. I passed a few slow moving vehicles on the long straight stretches. Immediately to the left were mountains - on one I saw a single tree standing in the center of a clear cut. To the right were fields of ripening blueberry bushes and long green grass and occasional assemblies of black and white dairy cows, lazy in the sun. Just past that there were more farms and then the dike and then the river.

I crossed over the Dewdney Slough, entering the hills that lead into the Upper Fraser Valley. I passed the Sasquatch Inn. The sun reflected off the Harrison River and I had to keep my eyes on the road.

I accelerated up Mt Woodside. I followed the highway, peering out to the right at the river far below and the mountains that started in after that.

I worked just a little further away in a community center in the sleepy town of Agassiz, about an hour and a half from Vancouver. For the better part of the shift I was alone. I had Internet, a view of the parking lot and beyond it the face of Mt. Cheam.

I had it down. I knew who would come in the door at any given time. I knew the range of behaviors to expect. I knew who would bitch. I knew who would complain and who would have something nice to say. I took people's gym membership cards. I answered their questions about upcoming programs. I cringed when the old ladies came for belly dancing Thursday nights in their jingly costumes. I forced a smile. I preferred the quiet days.

I don't remember feeling any satisfaction. Now and then, I'd suggest ways to make the place run a little better. Mostly, I did as little as possible.

At the end of the night I waited for Peter, the old Native Canadian janitor, to arrive so I could begin shutting everything down.

He'd been there since before I had. I saw him every night I worked without fail. I said a final goodbye to him knowing he'd be there cleaning up long after I'd gone.

"Good luck over there," he said.

"Thank you," I replied. "It's been a pleasure. Take it easy, eh."

I walked to my car. The parking lot was empty. I looked up at Mt. Cheam. It always felt much closer at night. Under the clear sky, I felt as if I could almost place my hand on it.

I fired up my car and a pr and then I was back on the road over the train tracks and back on the highway - free.

Descending from Mt. Woodside into Harrison Mills, I entered a trance. At the same place and time almost every night during my commute home I'd slip into it.

I looked down from high above. The Fraser River flashed silver, cutting through everything. Long lines of red and white lights, surrounded by black, trailed off in all directions. Over Vancouver I began moving higher at an escalating speed. I felt a deep chill as I passed the large buildings and bridges and the lights of the north shore.

And then I was above the ocean off the west coast of Vancouver Island. There I straightened out a little and came back a little closer to earth.

The moon was the only light. Its solid beam illuminated the white foam at the crest of each wave. In the center the reflection was blinding.

The dream evaporated as I slowed to cross the railroad tracks at the Dewdney Slough. As suddenly as it arrived, it was gone.

My parents saw me off at YVR. There wasn't much for us to say that hadn't already been said. I was going to Korea to teach English for a year. I turned around once to wave goodbye. I figured they deserved at least that.

I was surprised at how quickly I was boarding the plane. There was no turning back. It was to be the longest flight of my life. Floating above the Pacific Ocean at many thousands of feet for the next ten hours was hard to get past. It helps if you haven't googled the airline's safety record.

On take off I listened for tail scrape. Peering out the window I made a calculation to determine exactly the point a crash would be fatal. The truth is, once the cabin door is closed, your life is out of your hands.

I had to connect in San Francisco. I'd always wanted to see California, but not like this. In the terminal people moved quickly, with an exacting randomness. They walked in straight lines with their heads up. I had a little time before the big flight. I had a bite to eat, a final cheeseburger and fries. While I ate I looked out across the tarmac and wondered what might be beyond the horizon.

After, I pulled out my laptop and searched for news on Korea. The North was reaching out to the United States for food and fuel and in return they said they'd consider shutting down their nuclear reactor located at a facility called Yongbyon. The South was ferrying thousands of tons of fuel to its poorer, belligerent neighbor. Iran was being pressured to stop its pursuit of nuclear energy. Typhoons, tornadoes and earthquakes struck parts of the world I didn't know. There was a report that Al Quaeda had regrouped to a point not observed since 2001. Barry Bonds was suspected of juicing.

There was a report that China was banning the use of diethylene glycol, an industrial solvent used in paint and antifreeze, in its toothpastes. Countries around the world had taken action by stopping the toothpaste at their borders. I'd already packed enough tubes of Colgate to last the year.

I made my way to the gate as the time for my final departure drew near. Outside, I could see part of the big blue bird that would take me across the ocean. It glistened.

Inside, sprinkled in the hundreds of black haired men, woman and children were young bright-eyed Westerners who, I assumed, were there for the same purpose as me – adventure.

I had a conversation with my mom many months before, as I drove her to YVR for a business trip. I told her I was considering going to Asia to teach.

I didn't have much of a plan. I would escape for a little while. I would see things I hadn't thought about. And then I would see more.

She said, "I've always been impressed by people who did that."

She never left home. She had children. Her and my dad spent their adult lives working and driving us to sports after school.

I looked forward to the challenge of teaching. I hoped I'd find a little culture along the way. I also hoped to meet some interesting people. I had no clue what I'd see, really.

"Just promise you'll come back," she said.

"Of course I will," I answered.

A few weeks after graduating from university, I made a long awaited trip to the Bahamas to see Stew, my closest friend. I hadn't seen him for over a year.

He drove a new silver convertible Mini Cooper down the island highway while I looked out at the bright blue ocean and the pure white sand.

"It could rain at any time," he said.

There were bands of ominous cloud, but I wasn't worried.

After I dropped off my bags we went out to get supplies. We stopped at the Atlantis Hotel to get cigars. A tiny old fellow sat at a little table in the corner of the tobacco shop rolling them. They were soft and fresh and smelled sweeter than apple pie and I couldn't help salivating.

Then we stopped at a liquor store. He said he knew a real good Pinot Grigio. Typically I preferred red, but after a few bottles I couldn't argue.

We sat on the dock at the property he was taking care of. We talked a little about the future and about the trip I was going to take. I watched all the little fish swimming below. There was a menacing barracuda that hung around and Stew said that's the way it was.

He told me that he'd had a great time the last few weeks. He'd gone to the opening of a new resort a week before called the Cove at the Hotel. He saw celebrities. He told me about seeing Spike Lee, Janet Jackson and Steven Tyler from Aerosmith. He said he also saw Lindsay Lohan.

He fretted because the weather wasn't perfect. Scanning the dark clouds, he said, "What the hell? I'm sorry man. It hasn't been like this – *ever*. The last month was one of the nicest I've seen here."

When the heavy rain started, we moved under cover, carrying our wine. Looking back, there was a trail of cigar smoke in the heavy air.

"That's okay... Let's just drink – think it over."

"But, what do you want to do?" he asked.

"Take me somewhere nice."

"We *are* somewhere nice."

"Then let's just sit here."

It was balmy. Clouds moved slowly overhead, I couldn't think of a strong synonym to describe how bright they were. It rained from time to time and then the sun came out and it was golden. The pool was blue and electric yellow and we'd jump in now and then to cool off. After, we'd slosh back to our wine.

The next day we made it over to Harbor Island. We caught a flight over to Eleuthra Island, home of, supposedly, the best pineapples on earth. From there we took a tiny aluminum water-taxi to our destination.

We split at the dock. He had to handle some business. I made my way alone down a sandy path to the beach. Once there, I sat and closed my eyes for a little while. Everything was silent aside from the trembling of the waves

We met for breakfast overlooking the beach, but I could barely eat. I was thrown off by the weather. It was extremely muggy. I could do nothing to alleviate the sickness. I tried to soldier through. I managed to eat a little slice of pineapple and it was quite good.

It might've been unbearable if it wasn't for the air that was stirred up as we motored around the island in the all-terrain, golf cart that Stew procured. Before long I could enjoy some of the Heinekens we picked up from a little shack on a little hill where outside all around filthy chickens stepped about. After a few of them, I was all right.

Back in the little village, we ate 'The Best Conch Salad in the World.' We sat on a little terrace watching the owner dice up meat from a conch shell along with onion, tomato and green pepper. Then he added a dash of salt, a little hot pepper and some fresh lime juice.

"There you go," he said.

"Looks great," I said.

"My pleasure,"

Behind the restaurant you can see a pile of spent conch shells. In the distance I could see Eleuthra Island. It was getting on in the day and the sun wasn't quite as intense and with all the cloud it was almost pleasant.

"You should see this place during Junkanoo," Stew said, shaking his head slowly. "Get's packed."

I didn't know if he was serious.

We decided it was best to hop on the last flight. When we arrived back in Nassau we gave one of Stew's associates a ride into the city. He told us a little about living on the island. He said he'd seen a few things - Haitian refugees turned back by the Bahamian Coast Guard with machine gun fire, a colony of fabulously wealthy inbred white supremacist fisherman.

I didn't know about any of that, either.

He told Stew that work was coming along well, but the laborers were relentless in their effort to put off doing any work. He shook his head, "That's just the way it is here."

I wondered what my friend was doing down here. It wasn't that I thought he was shady. It wasn't that.

It was strange to think about him in this context. The path his life had taken made me have imaginings. I've always wondered what really went on.

Another day back in Nassau we took out the boat. I swam wearing only goggles and flippers. With the flippers I could race around looking at the reef up close. Now and then I'd see tropical fish I'd never dreamed of seeing. On one dive I spotted another barracuda. It sat, suspended in the water like a suspicious neighbor. I didn't see any sharks though Stew told me they were around.

While I was swimming, the wind picked up. He said it was impossible to keep the boat steady. He didn't want to wreck the reef, so he couldn't drop the anchor. For a while, he was nervous because he lost sight of me. I told him I kept my eye out, but I understood what he was trying to say. No one wants to cut a friend into ribbons.

Later on, we picked up a few of his friends and took a tour around Paradise Island. We passed around a bottle of wine. There were cruise ships docked along the shore next to the tiny downtown. Stew pointed out Nicholas Cage's island home. Then, we passed the giant Atlantis Resort and tied up in the harbor for dinner.

One night we drove into town to get Bertha's Famous GO-GO Ribs. As we ate, Stew asked me if I had my hepatitis shot.

"Not yet, no," I answered.

"Enjoy."

I added one more thing to my to-do list for Korea.

On the way back we took a brief tour. I'd never seen anything like it. I had never seen people living in such squalor.

"Guns. Drugs. Violence. Government Corruption. Goes on and on." Stew said.

I slouched down a little in the passenger seat.

Before long we were over the bridge. On Paradise Island giant yachts were anchored around the Atlantis Hotel. Stew said he'd seen much larger a few weeks before. Walking through the grounds, folks came out from the shadows offering all sorts of delights. It was the last thing I needed after what I'd experienced on the short drive around the other side.

Years before, Stew told me that his grandfather went to Korea to fight in the war when he was only sixteen years old. He heard him speak about the experience one or two times, but not in great detail. His grandfather said he was shocked to find himself in a real war when he arrived. It didn't take long to realize that he could easily be killed. He fought the Chinese and North Koreans in all types of conditions he would never

—

8

be comfortable in again. He never went camping in Canada after he returned. He said he'd done enough of that in Korea.

I asked Stew why his grandfather decided to fight in a war in a country that he couldn't have known much about. He said he didn't really know why.

Maybe people back then thought they could make a difference. I would need a pretty damn good reason to fight in a place that wasn't my home.

Obviously, I knew my experience wouldn't turn out the same way. But, I knew teaching jobs in Korea could also be a kind of hell. I'd read about more than a few horror stories.

I knew that children could be a pain in the ass. I'd certainly gone to great lengths to be one for many of my teachers. We'd gone to school together from the start. Both of us got booted out for one thing or another and gone back and roared through university. We'd come a long way.

He was happy for me. He might've been more enthusiastic than I was. He knew a little about what it felt like to escape. He told me he loved the island life. He said it would be hard to return to Canada.

3

After the Bahamas I left, almost immediately, on a fishing trip with my father, brother and various uncles and cousins, to our regular spot in the wilds of Northern Saskatchewan at a place called Wolf Lake.

The drive up is something else. It's no place to get lost or to have a breakdown. It's as Farley Mowat as I will likely ever get. Flin Flon, Manitoba is the closest city, but I've never been there. It is a few hours further and we always have everything we need packed away. Typically, we'd bring far too much.

My brother, who was living in Ottawa at the time while he articled to become a lawyer, brought his mentor, the Judge. The Judge was a respected fellow in his field. He sat on the bench of the Supreme Court of Canada. He was French Canadian. He loved to fish. He'd spring for wine. He fit right in, as far as I was concerned.

I think my dad brought the two of us out so he could connect with us the way he did with his dad.

He loved being out in a boat with friends and family, but not just anyone. He only brought people who could cast a decent line.

You were only allowed one mistake. If for any reason you wound up with a bird's nest, he'd let loose an unvarying barrage of expletives I can't repeat. You learned not to let your line get hung up.

The first year my brother, my dad and I made the voyage I couldn't do anything right. Even when I knew my rig was working, the fish just didn't bite. They told me to try harder. They got a real kick out of that.

My dad grew up in a large family and he moved away at very young age to pursue his dream of playing pro hockey. He grew up in a little dirt town in the middle of nowhere, Saskatchewan. He felt the impulse to leave as sure as I did, probably more.

He was a decent goalie. He played in the WHL. He got to travel a fair bit throughout the States in minor league towns. He had a cup of coffee with the old California Golden Seals.

He told me about his glory days. He told me he would've made it if there were as many teams then as there are now.

My dad did get to see a childhood friend raise the Stanley Cup. He played for the NY Islanders when they clinched the cup in Vancouver. Every time we'd go in to see a game at the Pacific Coliseum he'd point at where he was sitting during the cup-clinching game. As a kid, I ate it all up.

As I said, he made it pretty far for a smaller than average player, but he gave it up for steadier work and, after that, a family. Lucky for me he never made it.

He always made a spectacle of catching a fish, no matter the size. You knew immediately when he had a fish hooked. He couldn't conceal his excitement. He'd stand up and lift his rod. He'd rock the boat. Never patient, always in great haste, he'd command one of us to get the net.

He'd say, "Get the net!"

I failed to scoop a fair-sized fish he hooked early on and it got away. I listened to his lament for over a decade. I didn't miss many after, but I know for a while he wondered why he'd been cursed with such a nitwit for a son.

He'd stand on the bow of the red and grey aluminum fishing boat we'd rent from the resort. With the engine cut, the silent wild breathes into you and it passes on something that cannot be explained.

Eventually one of his casts into the lily pads would be answered and he'd turn and look down at us with a smile and blazing eyes: "Got one!"

It was the most alive I've ever seen the man.

On nice days, you can't wait to get out on the water. The first beer comes soon after catching the day's first fish. Even on cool mornings it didn't take long before a few cans were clanking around at your feet.

My uncles had me mix Caesars when we came in for the day while they prepared dinner. I've been working on pouring the perfect Caesar for most of my adult life. I put celery salt on the rim of each glass and made sure each drink had a healthy amount of ice. Vodka. More Vodka. 3-4 fingers. Clamato Juice. Tabasco. Worcestershire. Lemon. Spicy pickled green bean.

All the while we'd stand by the fire, shooting the breeze. We always caught lots of fish - each one a story. The alcohol never stopped flowing. All the words blended with the faces and the flames and the shadows and the smoke.

After a while everyone begins to take on a Saskatchewan accent and every sentence ends, "Jesus Christ" (Though, I don't believe I heard those words spoken by the Judge).

Around the fire you would occasionally meet others staying at the resort. I've met good people at Wolf Lake from as far away as Florida. A fellow from down there showed us a few spots on the lake that he knew about. He was probably the only guy more enthusiastic than my dad.

When he heard I was heading to Korea he told me to stay away from 'the kimchi.'

I knew almost nothing about Korean cuisine. I couldn't think of any Korean dish. I assumed there would be a lot of rice. I didn't mind rice.

He said, "It's not all bad. I just don't like *that* stuff."

He said he ate Korean BBQ when he was a student living in New York.

He said while he lived there he killed a man that tried to enter his apartment through a window. The bullet ripped through the center of the guy's forehead. When the police arrived afterward one of the officers said to him, "Nice shot."

Jesus Christ.

On the lake there are giant eagles, bald ones and golden ones, that sit high on treetops along the shore. Every now and then you see one take off. There are giant pelicans white like clouds with beaks orange like pencils. Sometimes you see healthy black bears climbing on the steep rocky shore. One time we disturbed one taking a shit in the summer sun and the poor son-of-a-bitch scrambled up the rock face so quick it neglected to squeeze it off. We were all astonished at how much shit came out of it.

On cloudless days big planes leave long white lines across the sky. We'd joke about an old elementary school teacher who became obsessed with chemtrails. That was about the only reminder of the outside.

From the lake, you can see where forest fires burned. Huge tracts of land are barren except for random trees that have somehow been spared.

In the winter everything freezes, but I've never experienced that, thankfully.

There were people that lived here year round. They were mostly Native Canadians from a place called Pelican Bay, a little community further up the lake.

The first person that I came across from the area had a job cleaning fish. My uncle – also named Dan – was aghast at people who allowed their catch to be filleted (or butchered, as he said was done) by people like him. Anyway, I came across him, in the cleaning station, as he showed my uncle the deep purple bruise that ran from his shoulder down his backside.

"The hell?" I said.

"Fight," the guy answered.

"Who won?"

"Don't remember," he said.

My uncle turned away, shaking his head. He pulled out a fish and slid his knife into it and then he ripped out all the gore and threw it in a garbage can. I turned and meandered back to the dock to gather the rest of the gear, so I could get to mixing drinks.

That first year my brother and I came, we went to the bar at the Minoquay Hotel. It was a total dive, but there was little else to explore after the older folk went to sleep.

It wasn't late and the fire was warm. It never got dark. You can see clear for miles down the lake in the middle of the night. Occasionally you were reminded where you were: there'd be a howl from somewhere deep in the woods, or a loon might decide to let out a few of its indescribable notes, carried along the water.

I'm not totally sure, but I think he convinced me to take a walk over and have a beer with the locals. It was only a short walk.

There was little to speak of inside the bar. There was smoke. The floor stuck to my feet. There were hard wood tables, chairs and a crooked old red felt pool table. There were enough people so that you could hear voices over the sound of the Def Leopard.

He bought a round. I bought another. I was coming back with a few more bottles when he grabbed me by the elbow and said with an understated urgency, "Time to leave."

We stepped outside and walked down the road back to our cabin. I asked him what happened.

He said, "You saw that guy I was talking with? He lives around here. He told me his brother was murdered a few years earlier."

"Terrible," I answered.

"So I ask him. What happened to the guy that killed him," he continued. "So he nods toward a guy sitting at the bar, "That's him over there.'"

We continued walking back toward the fire. Beyond, at the bottom of the sky, where it met the lake, there was a thin line of silver.

It likely won't change anytime soon. I remember when the conversation came around to the people who lived around it, the Judge said, "There is no such thing as justice."

That week, we drank the Minoquay out of red wine. We caught our limit. I wondered when I would return.

4

My last excursion in North America was a trip across the border to watch a ball game in Seattle with a cousin, Jack. The Mariners were playing the Blue Jays Canada Day weekend. We left early on Friday.

I knew very little about Seattle. I had never spent more than a few days there in my life. Before that, the last time I went to watch a ball game there, the M's were playing in the King Dome, Ken Griffey Jr. was still 'The Kid' and I knew nothing of Nirvana.

There were no home runs. Most of the game I waited in line for beer. I don't remember who won. Big planes, making their descent into Seatac Airport, passed overhead.

After the game we collected ourselves a little. We agreed we might not make it through the border in our condition. It was a long drive. We had to sober up. A border guard might catch us with one of their Jedi mind tricks.

We turned south to look for a hotel near Seatac Airport. We couldn't find anything. Every hotel we checked was full. We decided to try our luck a little further south. We took a wrong exit and ended up back at the same strip of hotels we'd just come from.

Our first time around we didn't try the Hilton. We weren't looking to spend lots of money on a room. However, this time we had no choice.

Jack went inside. He came out quickly. I didn't want to consider having to sleep in his truck. As he came closer, I noticed he had a smile. He held up a key.

"There's a little conference, but we got a room."

"Yeah," I answered. "Can you reach the beer?"

"The lounge is open," he said.

"Is it?"

He passed a can. He said, "We'll need a couple drinks."

Of course I'd need a drink.

We got to our room, cleaned up and headed back to the main building. There was something strange about him.

He pounded a can on the walk across the parking lot. As we got closer to the entrance he choked a little.

"Everything all right?" I asked.

He didn't answer.

From outside the glass doors I looked down the hall. Inside, little people were walking everywhere. There were a few normal sized people, at least enough for comparison's sake.

"Where are we?"

I opened the door and walked in. It was a typical franchise hotel down to the blue and green patterned carpet and soft light - nothing special to see at all except for the smattering of tiny humans. Here two, there four, that way another four or five. They were everywhere.

My cousin was doubled over in the shadows, crying he was laughing so hard. He was shaking. I thought he was going to throw up. He had to take a knee.

"A drink." I said, holding open the door, stunned. I couldn't believe he held it in that long.

He barely made it in. He slipped behind an alcove. He needed more time.

It was surreal. I didn't know if we would make it to the lounge not 100 feet away.

A family walked past us. There were two large parents and two little kids. The little kids were teenagers. They came up to my hip.

More and more streamed passed us. They exited a large conference hall. Here and there, average sized folk stood out like tall trees in a landslide.

I pretended to tie my shoe. I looked through the parade of little legs to catch a glimpse of my cousin pretending to talk on his phone.

After everyone filtered passed we walked down the hall to the lounge. We were both on edge, obviously.

17

The lounge was filled with little people. Somehow we maintained enough to order drinks. We managed to find a quiet table. Before long, we made friends with a little dude.

"You had no idea you'd be drinking at Willy Wonka's tonight did you boys?" He asked. "Want some chocolate?"

Jack choked on his drink. I looked up at the young waitress who stood there to take our order. Her eyes were massive. Her legs shook. I started laughing. The laughter was contagious.

I looked around the lounge. I tried to imagine all the strange things I'd seen in my life. There was nothing to do except order another drink and try to remember everything.

The little guy understood. "I work in Las Vegas," he said. "I've seen some crazy shit - I totally understand. But *this*, I dream about *this*. I've never been around this many people like me in my life. I am going to get silly - see that girl?" He nodded toward a table at the far end of the lounge. He gave us a wink.

He told us about the Little People of America, the group that put on the event. He was a new member. It was his first conference. I told him I would google it when I got back to Canada.

The next day my cousin and I sat in a Denny's eating a fine American breakfast. I looked for little people, but I didn't see any there.

We stayed across the line another day recovering. We thought about seeing another ball game, but then thought better of it. We ended up drinking Jagermeister and Red Bull cocktails next to a pool at a hotel a little closer to the border.

On the trip across the Pacific I had the window, but I couldn't see much of anything. The first few hours I watched the electronic map trace the plane's path. We flew so close to Vancouver I felt a little irritated. I wondered why I had to go to San Francisco.

It was a free flight. A plane ticket was e-mailed to me by the manager as soon as the Korean Consulate processed my visa. While it was frustrating having to spend an extra six hours in airports and airplanes, everything was pretty uneventful.

I was in and out of sleep. Whenever I needed to go to the washroom I had to step over identical twin brothers about ten years of age. I rethought asking for the window seat. There was a hair in one of my meals, a beef, vegetable and rice dish with sweet red pepper sauce. Now and then I'd turn on the screen to watch the plane's course. First, we passed to the south of Alaska. Then, we were to the south of Russia. Finally we passed over the little nub of land I'd be living in for the year. Eventually we were told to prepare for our final descent. As we circled far above, I saw life below on the islands in the tidal flats off the west coast of the peninsula.

We arrived at Incheon Airport as the sun started to set. The flight across the Pacific was delayed a little and I had another flight to catch immediately upon arriving, so I was a curious mixture of tired and frantic. As things seem to go in these situations I picked the slow moving line to have my passport stamped.

The line shuffled slowly. Everything was out of my hands. After my passport was stamped, I ran to the domestic departures terminal. I had three bags; a backpack filled with a laptop and other vital supplies; a large bag stuffed with clothes, a few books, a year supply of razors and Old Spice

19

deodorant; and a bag filled with freshly disinfected hockey gear.

I had to pick up my sticks at the over-sized luggage desk. I taped about ten together so when I got to play some puck I could sell a few to those who needed them. Where I'd play I wasn't sure, but I had talked to a few people already in Daegu and they assured me it was on.

I pushed the cart, stacked with my luggage, through the terminal. Passing thru sliding double doors the sticks caught on both sides. The doors rattled. Folks lifted their heads to have a look. I didn't need to wear a maple leaf.

Reaching the domestic departure terminal with minutes to spare I checked in for my final flight. I checked my bags and headed to the gate.

Unfortunately, as soon as I got there I was sent back. I was directed to a room adjacent to the check in counter where I was told to open my luggage. The X-ray spotted something suspicious. As it turns out, three canisters of Gillette shaving cream packed away in my bag set off an alarm. The Customs lady told me I must throw away two of the three canisters.

I wondered why. Why not throw all the canisters out? Why do I get to keep one? The cans made it all the way from Vancouver and now they're a problem? There wasn't much to do. See you later shaving cream, hello Korea.

6

The plane shot down the runway. It took off clean. It ascended, making a large turn away from the North. Almost immediately I was looking down at the lights of Seoul, the nation's Capital.

Through the window on the far side, I could see a flaming red dusk. Out the window next to me, under my tired eyes, lay the sparkling neon night of South Korea.

Despite how tired I felt, I looked out the window the entire way to Daegu. I could see large clusters of lights that made up the suburbs of Seoul. From so far above everything looked rather orderly. As we descended into Daegu I began to make out objects on the ground. Through the whipping clouds, I could make out highways and buildings and glowing green artificial turf soccer fields.

I had studied for weeks where I would be going, but I couldn't get any bearing now being delirious from the long hours spent in the air.

Finally the plane touched down. I couldn't believe I'd actually arrived. I could have been anywhere.

The airport in Daegu was a little less impressive than the one in Seoul. The domestic arrival building was blue and official. The baggage area was musty. Stepping outside the arrival gates with my bags I was greeted by a solid wall of humid air.

A fellow from the school met me.

"Daniel?" he enquired.

"Yes," I said. There didn't seem to be any other Daniels on the flight. "You are with the Young Shoes English School?" I asked.

"Yes. Come," he said gesturing toward the parking lot. He took one of my bags and we were off. As it turns out, he was an assistant to the owner of the school. I was told later the two were somehow related.

I chose to work in a *hagwon*, a private English language academy that operates after regular school. It wasn't a hard decision: the hours were short, I could sleep in every day and it paid more than a public school.

I was working one Sunday morning at the community center when I had the interview. The lady who recruited me was from Alberta. She said she had just finished a contract with the school and was now back home in Canada attending school to get her Master's degree in ESL.

She said the school wasn't looking for a teacher with experience, just someone who was adventurous, motivated and willing to commit to a year. She said she liked that I had taught children's swimming lessons and that I had a background in History.

She sent me a link to a video of the manager. In the video he was making chicken curry with coconut milk. She also said that the owner was a Christian. I didn't know what that meant. It certainly wasn't a deciding factor for me.

I looked at other jobs and talked to a handful of recruiters, but I felt comfortable talking to this lady and was reassured by the knowledge that she was a former employee. Also, she was a little older, she sounded sweet and she was able to answer every question I had. I knew it was the best of what I was being offered.

I felt something was a little off with most of the recruiters and schools that answered when I posted my resume on the Dave's ESL Café website.

After I foolishly left my phone number for anyone to see, I was answering calls from unknown area codes at all hours. It wasn't pleasant reaching for the phone at 3am to hear: *"Herro. This is Mr. Ree!"*

Within 12 hours of posting my resume online, my inbox was flooded with offers. I didn't answer the recruiters who wanted me to sign a contract quickly. I talked to a few who became startlingly evasive when I asked for pictures of the school, most wouldn't called back.

In the end, I found it extremely difficult to trust any of the middlemen and women who contacted me. They are paid to place you at a school. They might tell you they have a long relationship with a school. They might have a professional looking website. The truth is they try to send you to the schools that pay them the most.

Some of these schools are very desperate for one reason or another. Maybe one of their teachers left in the middle of the night. Maybe there was an emergency. You can't know for sure. I thought it best to avoid anything that didn't feel right.

The school that sponsors your visa has tremendous power over you. With an E-2 visa, the visa the vast majority of teachers are required to obtain, the holder cannot transfer to another school without their current school's permission. *Think about that.* The employer has to sign an official letter of release for the employee to change jobs. If the owner won't sign the release you have to leave the country or stay on working. If you haven't been in country longer than six months you have to reimburse the school for the plane ticket they paid for to bring you over. You also have to pay for a ticket home.

Many people come over right after college - all wet and in debt. Shady school owners prey on these types. They squeeze everything they can out of you – more hours, work at different locations, late paychecks and, sometimes, verbal abuse. For young women it can get particularly nasty. No one wants to look like a failure. Often they'll just take it from the man.

I didn't want to be one of the horror stories. Speaking to this lady I felt confident I wouldn't be screwed around.

23

We got into the school's van and drove away from the airport into the city. It wasn't far off.

It was dark. There was a tropical feel because of the rain and the heat. It was the start of the rainy season. The rain came down aggressively. I am from the West Coast. I thought I knew rain.

The airport was near the center of the city; as we moved through traffic, I noticed a few familiar things. Through the rain streaked windows I could see the bright neon signs of a few multinational companies. Moving through the city I saw - McDonald's, Burger King, Adidas, and Baskin Robbins. There were multitudes of other shops I had never seen - The Red Face, Lotteria, Paris Baguette, and so on.

Everywhere there were people moving quickly under umbrellas. From what I could make out, they were nicely dressed. By all appearances there was nothing too foreign. If forced to describe my initial impression of Daegu in a word, I would call it simply 'modern.'

The rain continued as we made our way across town. We took a bypass onto an expressway. Then, we took a bridge over a wide river. Next, we coasted through a small bright suburb and up a hill.

The driver and I exchanged a few words.

"Korea. Wow."

"Yes."

"Lots of lights."

"Yes!"

"Alright."

"Where you from?"

"Canada"

"Ahh, very nice"

"Yep, you bet"

"Ummm?"

"Uhhh, I mean, yes"

"Uhnnn... I want to learn English."

"I see..."

We shot through a tunnel. On the other side we reached a toll. He flipped a coin into it and we took the first exit down into the town. Arriving in Chilgok Area 3, I gave my eyes a little rub. The place was buzzing.

7

We passed another Baskin Robbins, turned, drove a little further and parked up on a sidewalk next to a building.

Outside, the air was thick and smoky. The rain had let up and now only random drops fell.

The driver directed me to a passage between a cluster of neon lights and a restaurant with several bright red glowing chickens revolving on a multi-pronged spit.

It wasn't any less humid in the building. I began to sweat through my shirt. I stepped into an elevator with the driver and a group of children all wearing matching green backpacks. More kids, with yellow backpacks, appeared from a different entrance. Most of them had hair matted to their foreheads. Mercifully, the doors closed before it could be filled any further. A few of the kids stared at me while others giggled.

On the fifth floor we got out, half the children emptied on the previous floor, going to another after-school operation. I learned later on that each building in the area was full of similar businesses specializing in one subject or other.

Stepping through the glass doors, I saw a bright, modern looking school. There were classrooms, desks and chairs and there was air conditioning. The rooms were all named after famous universities like Harvard, Yale and Princeton.

A teenage boy dragged his feet as he walked down a hallway. He gave me a quick sideways glance. The frown on his face gave way to a yawn. He looked like he wanted to be any place else.

I met the manager, Yoon. He was shorter, balder and stockier than I had envisioned. He wore a logoed t-shirt and cargo pants.

He said he wanted me to come to the school first and say hello before going to my apartment. He motioned me away from the entrance because I was damning back a school of students. I was zoned out. Nothing was registering, nor would it until I sat down or closed my eyes for a day or so. I think he must have realized it too.

A voice entered my head saying, *"Asia... Korea... What the hell are you doing?"*

He gave me the keys to the apartment and told me he'd come by before school the next day.

The driver and I went back down the elevator. At the bottom, more kids stood directly in front of the elevator doors, waiting to get in.

We got back in the van. I tried to follow where I was being taken, so I wouldn't get lost if I decided to go for a walk. We rounded one corner and another toward our destination.

A minute later, we stopped at a convenience store. I would frequent this particular place, as it turned out to be quite close to my apartment. It was one of four corner stores within a minute of my front door that I shopped at, depending on what I needed. Water was cheaper at once place; another carried nacho cheese chips; another place had a better selection of fruits and vegetables.

From this store I could see a few restaurants, a bike shop, a video rental store and a bakery. They were all still open. I wouldn't need to walk far for anything.

Inside I saw, to my surprise, an American girl. I managed a hello as I squeezed by her through the narrow aisle. I mentioned to her I'd just arrived. I think she might've been caught off guard to see another foreigner, fresh off the boat.

It was hard to take in anything at that point, but I wanted to see if I could find something familiar. Walking through the store I saw some items I recognized and others I didn't. I estimated I could get by without having to adjust too much.

I grabbed a few cans of Budweiser, a blue box of cereal flakes, with what looked to be Tony the Tiger on the front, and some milk. I also bought a bag of chips that turned out to be a rancid seafood flavor.

I paid and stepped outside. I walked out into the rain, got into the van and we accelerated off down the narrow road to my apartment a few hundred feet around a corner. On the way, we passed several more restaurants. There were tanks with fish, squid, mollusks and other strange creatures I couldn't name.

The driver wedged his ride into the tiniest of spaces. As we collected my luggage, an old lady, who turned out to be my neighbor, greeted me. I bowed to her and gave her a smile. She said something unintelligible. It struck me pretty hard then just where I was. I looked at all the cars lining the narrow street. I looked down the rows of apartments; up and beyond, I could make out some of the same stars I saw back home.

She dropped the cigarette she was smoking and turned to go inside her apartment. I noticed behind her open door, stacked to the roof, many large orange bags full of onions.

Before she closed her door, she said something else to the driver.

"What did she say?" I asked him.

"She said - you learn Korean."

For the first little bit I was smoking Swisher Sweets I'd brought from home. I would go downstairs and stand by the entrance to the apartment and have a smoke. When she was outside she'd sometimes light my cigars for me with her old hands.

She made me think of my own grandmother. The last thing she said to me, on hearing I was going to Korea, was, "Don't marry one of them."

She must have seen her share of strange things. I tried to be as kind to her as I could, despite the awkwardness I felt at my inability to communicate the simplest thoughts.

Anyway, we wrestled my bags up three flights of stairs, opened the door, and walked into a surprisingly spacious two bedroom flat.

There were a few unmistakable signs of passion or struggle. There were curious indents in the front door. There was a bare blue mattress lying in the spare bedroom.

I pointed to the door and the guy shrugged and said, "Sorry."

At this point I wasn't questioning.

My first thought was that the flat was roomy; it had two decent sized bedrooms. Because it also had a desk, the room with the mattress became my office. The whole place was relatively clean. All in all, I was pretty happy with the place.

The driver showed me how to turn on the hot water. Any time I wanted to use it I had to press a button.

Then he left. I stood for a while, finally not compelled to move.

Outside, it was raining again. There was a glowing neon-orange cross on the roof of the building opposite mine.

I opened a cold Budweiser and stood at an open window breathing the smoky night air. I was too tired to think. I went to the bedroom. I stretched out on the bed. The mattress was rigid.

Hanging from the ceiling was a pink plastic pig with angel wings, another strange leftover from the former occupant. I was sleeping in the baby's room. And for the first night at least I would sleep like one.

I woke up and found the bedroom light on and there was a copy of *The Razor's Edge* by W. Somerset Maugham wresting on my chest.

I got up to turn the light off. There was a faint light coming through the windows - a new dawn. I stepped toward it and took in the view.

8

At about noon I received a phone call from Yoon. He asked how everything was. I told him the apartment was roomier than I expected. I thanked him for having everything set up. He said he'd be right over. I gathered myself and found my key. I hadn't been outside yet.

On our walk, he told me a little about himself. He said he had travelled a lot as a kid. He attended high school in India. He used to sing in a heavy metal band. He seemed to be a passionate guy.

You could see his eyes light up when he spoke. He said he was concerned about the environment. As we walked down the sidewalk, lined with wilting red roses, he mentioned how he didn't see as many insects now as he did when he was as a kid. He wondered what had happened to everything. He said things like that were his motivations for teaching.

I knew right away that I wouldn't have too many issues with him. Despite our different nationalities we shared a lot of similar ideas. It was a tremendous relief.

It was hard to ignore all of the massive off-white apartment blocks. Each had a random number and a pleasant graphic of a butterfly or grasshopper or some other happy image pasted in a pastel shade, half way up its side. Even at midday, they cast long shadows.

There were an awful lot of people moving about. They were mostly woman and young children, though a few older folks were sprinkled in. On the sidewalk there were tents and little blue pickup trucks selling fresh fruit and vegetables. There seemed to be a lot of traffic, too. Taxis, scooters and motorcycles shot down the streets.

I tried to remember the route we were taking. We had been walking for only ten minutes, but I don't think I could have found my way back. I didn't know quite how far we were walking and I didn't know in which direction. It was a different way than I was taken the previous day.

We passed a public school. As we waited at an intersection close by, a large group of children suddenly formed. I was hit with a barrage of smiling 'hellos' and 'nice to meet yous.'

I assumed they were just let out. They were all in different uniforms. In the heat, their hair was matted to their sweaty brows.

We passed a 7/11 and crossed a broad, modern looking road. On the other side we entered an all-you-can-eat BBQ buffet. My shirt was beginning to stick to my back.

I thought it was nice of Yoon to take me out and also give me a day to get my bearings. He could've said I was to start teaching right then, but he had another fellow there to cover the day's classes.

He tried to educate me about Korean food. I tried to listen. It tasted great. I wasn't used to eating garlic at lunch, but I managed to pack some away, as it seemed to be the thing to do.

I tried to communicate my excitement to have the opportunity to teach and to tell him I was looking forward to finally starting. I didn't quite know what to say.

We finished and made our way to the school. I never went back to that restaurant again, though I passed it almost daily before it went out of business a little later on. At the time, there were quite a few all you can eat BBQ restaurants like this one.

We walked back through the town down the middle of the road, because there were cars parked all over the sidewalks.

Everything in this part of Chilgok seemed to be new or in the process of being built. Each building was eerily similar to the next. Each street was also very similar. I could see how it was easy to get lost in all the sameness.

Yoon told me that he lived on the other side of the city. He didn't spend a lot of time in Chilgok. He said it was strange to see so much construction. It wasn't like this elsewhere in Daegu.

He said, "Ten years ago this was rice fields."

We made it back to the school and I was given a full tour. There were classrooms, a media room, a lunchroom, and a large staff room.

The staff room was filled with desks, but there were only two teachers. The school was built with the hope of expanding. I would have lots of space to prepare at least.

Along with desks and chairs, the main feature of each classroom was a large LCD monitor used to play DVDs that each child received as part of their enrolment. Each DVD contained a month's worth of lessons that we covered in the classroom.

He told me there were enough lessons to last 6 months, after six months children graduated to the next level. As a result, I would get to see each lesson two times. I immediately thought how this would eliminate preparation for the last 6 months.

Then, he asked if I smoked.

"Cigars, occasionally," I said.

"I'm going to have a smoke. Join me."

We walked down a long hallway. He stopped and pointed out the washrooms. There was a musty, stale odor, but there was a toilet. I confirmed that before coming over.

He opened a door at the end of the hallway, stepping out and motioning me to close the door after I'd come through.

We were in an unused stairwell.

"Gotta be careful mothers don't see me light up."

"Ah."

"So that's the school," he said, smiling as he puffed on a long, thin cigarette. He caught me looking at it.

"Long," I said.

"It's a menthol."

I smiled.

"So what's the plan for today, Yoon?"

"You're free for now, Daniel. Do you like to be called Daniel?"

"Sure, Daniel, Dan - either way's fine."

He took another drag.

I took a second to look at where we were. Down the stairs, I saw a couple full garbage bags and some dusty furniture. I looked up and saw desks, broken chairs, and dead trees wrapped in colorful ribbons stacked to the ceiling.

He said, "You can go out, but be back at 6pm or so. I want you to observe a lesson. Presentation class. Students come up to the front of the room and speak. You help them with pronunciation."

"No problem. What time is it?" I asked.

"Almost three."

"Is it okay if I go for walk?"

"Sure, where're you going to go?"

"Just for a look around. I'll try not to get lost," I added with a smile.

"Good. See you later."

I made my way out throwing high fives at a few bewildered children.

I had to go by the reception desk. The secretary smiled as I passed by. A few mothers were there paying for books. I tried to smile and look serious. They smiled. I slowed down and said hello. They said hello. It was awkward for a few seconds and then I gave a slight bow and turned toward the door.

After that, I decided to keep a more comfortable distance. Next time I would give a hello in passing. No need for a full stop. It was easier for everyone if I just did a fly-by.

I opened the glass doors and stepped into the elevator. Once inside I took a deep breath. All in all things weren't so bad.

Outside it was hot. I traced my way through the streets, down to the 7/11 I saw before.

Looking for something to drink, I saw a strange mix of familiar and new. I reached for a Mountain Dew. At the counter I noticed a display with cigars similar to the one's I'd grown addicted to and I gestured to the lady behind the counter to include a pack. I smiled dumbly, not knowing how to explain my way through the simplest transaction. I'd have to do a little learning in my spare time.

I sat down at a plastic table and chairs with an umbrella and pulled out a fresh cigar. I puffed away, drinking a cold Mountain Dew, while taking in the scene.

Across from me was the restaurant where Yoon and I ate lunch. Beyond that I couldn't see much because a row of buildings stood in the way. To the left there was another building. To the right there were a few empty lots and further there were buildings under construction.

I didn't want to walk too far for fear of losing my way. I didn't want to be that guy. All things pointed to a long sit in the shade.

Between the restaurant and the 7/11 was an extremely wide boulevard. To where, I had no idea. For a good while I watched people line up at the crosswalk and carefully look for oncoming vehicles before walking across.

Not one car slowed. Sometimes people stood for minutes. Up until this point everything appeared to be a pretty decent facsimile of the world I knew. This was one of the first subtle tears in the illusion I had of Korea.

I took a mental note to be very careful when crossing the road.

It wasn't long before I noticed the sounds of golf balls clicking, as they were struck at random. The sound was coming from high above in a building on the other side of the road. Sure enough I saw a sign with a ball, club and a crown.

Just then I was startled by another aspect of Korea I hadn't counted on. A line of evenly spaced fighter jets roared

34

overhead. They shrieked by, one after the other. The noise echoed in the surrounding buildings. They came in so low I could almost read their markings.

I sat staring up at the six or seven that passed. It wasn't shocking to see or anything, just unexpected. Korea is still technically at war. I guessed that the planes belonged to the United States and that they were landing at the same airport I arrived at the night before.

I shrugged, dropped the cigar and stepped on it. The planes looked totally under control - nothing to see.

After a minute or so I found myself looking back at the crossing. I was far more concerned with it.

I followed the same way Yoon and I took after lunch, the same one I took to get to the 7/11. It was up to me to find my way back because I didn't know how to ask anyone where my school was located.

Around that time I noticed people glancing in my direction. This was another new experience. Usually back home I blended into the background without any problem. Back home I was a common height; I had a face with common features; and, as I drove a nondescript automobile, I could go about my business without attracting a second look. It looked as if I could forget about that. There weren't many second looks because the first ones were so long.

I was slightly lost, though the walk was short and I'd made no more than two changes of direction.

I knew the school was nearby. I scratched my head. I looked back down the street I had just passed and saw a landmark; a bright red and white and blue twirling barber pole, hanging from the side of my school's building. Looking up, I saw Young Shoes English School printed in yellow and green.

I went into the building, up the elevator and through the modern glass doors. There weren't any students around. It occurred to me school might be in session.

"Hi Daniel," Yoon said from somewhere in his office. "I want you to meet someone."

I walked through the foyer into his office and saw a thin, middle-aged woman.

"Hello. Pleased to meet you," I said, holding out my hand.

She gave me a cold limp handshake.

"My name is Daniel."

"Hello, My name is Ji Eun," she said with a nervous smile.

"Great. Nice to meet you."

"Where are you from?" she asked.

"Canada...Vancouver."

She smiled, "Ahh, Ban ku-ba."

"Yeah it's not too bad a place."

"Uhhn..."

"Oh, well, it's very nice to meet you."

"Uhuh..." she replied

Yoon cleared his throat and we turned to him. It looked like he wasn't going to be explaining anything so I took the opportunity to excuse myself.

"I'll just be in the staff room, if you need me," I said to Yoon.

"Sure," he replied, adding, "I'll come and get you to observe Darryl in a little while."

Ji Eun hurried out behind me into a classroom and closed the door behind her. A few girls in matching uniforms were standing at the classroom window peering out. I looked back at them, making a weird face and they held their hands over their mouths. I heard a voice come from behind the door and the girls rushed to their seats.

I sat down at a computer and typed a message for my parents. I didn't know quite what to say. It was a little overwhelming, but I was calm. The plane didn't crash. The North didn't invade. Everything was going to be okay.

There wasn't anything to do except wait for the bell to ring. I was a little anxious to meet some of the students. I made a cup of instant coffee and had a sip. It was *awfully* sweet stuff.

Darryl the substitute was not what I expected. He was a giant, African American fellow from Alabama. You could easily mistake him for a nose tackle. You'd never guess he was an English teacher.

He was sweating like someone had thrown a bucket of water on him. He gave a smile as if to say, "I know."

"Hi there," I said. "My name's Dan."

"Darryl," He said. His voice resonated like it came from a deep cavern.

I shook his hand and said, "Pleased to meet you."

He gave me a little look over. He must have wondered who the new guy could be, too.

"Ready to go?" he asked.

My first class was with students who had a few years of English learning under their belts. Most were in their last year of middle school.

There were four girls and a boy. You could tell right away that the girls controlled the class. The tall boy folded his arms and waited. You could tell he was a nice kid. The girls were, joking and laughing with each other as girls do.

I didn't start by ripping pages out of any textbooks. There were no textbooks.

I introduced myself. "Hello, my name is Daniel. What are your names?"

The group of girls gave their names one after the other.

"I'm Joanne."

"Sunny."

"Stella."

"Angel."

I turned to the boy surrounded by an ocean of empty desks.

"Jake." he said to me, raising his chin.

I took a second. I tried to think. Did they just…? Stella? Angel? It wasn't what I was expecting. I didn't have any idea what to say.

I turned to Darryl, a little perplexed. He was sitting, sorting papers waiting for the DVD to load so the lesson could begin.

I scratched my head.

Darryl, seeing that I was at a loss said, "They've all got English nicknames."

"I see."

He told me he had to step out for a moment. He said they were usually given a little while to prepare their presentations, so I just sat there. I looked at the clock. They all pulled out their electric dictionaries.

I decided to try to have a conversation with them.

"So what do you like to do?" I asked.

"Shopping."

"Shopping."

"Shopping."

"Shopping."

"Sleep," added Jake.

"Sleep?" I repeated "But you're young?"

"Yes... I like sleep."

"Okay… What are we doing here?" I said to no one in particular.

I moved to inspect some of their writing. Joanne was clearly the leader and her writing was easily the most impressive. I checked each student's writing. They weren't bad.

I have never had a great command of the terminology of the English language. I couldn't tell them their particles were misplaced or that they didn't use a correct clause or conjunction. I only knew what didn't sound or look correct, more or less.

I had to go back in time. I remember being in school on days you couldn't motivate me to write a single line. I once got

0% for an entire term of Creative Writing in high school. I was told I'd be on welfare when I grew up by my grade six teacher. My record was definitely suspect.

From the beginning these kids were a dream, relatively speaking. I wasn't working in a public school in Chicago or Northern Canada. It wasn't going to be hard time.

They were working on memorizing the scripts they'd arranged a few days before in their writing classes. I was in charge of that class as well. For the high level children I only had to worry about writing and presentation classes.

I looked at the bare walls and the cheap fluorescent lighting. I saw the computer sitting in the corner. I looked out the windows at the street below.

One of the girls asked, "Teacher, where are you from?"

I turned around. I replied, "I'm from Vancouver, Canada."

"Ah, Ban ku-ba."

Jake raised his head a little. He'd been scribbling away quietly. He looked comfortable in his desk.

"There are nice mountains," he said slowly and evenly.

"Yes, there are. Do you like skiing?" I asked.

"Yes teacher. Umm, I like snowboarding."

I was impressed. I could never snowboard. I had an accident when I was a kid, strapped to something from a Sears catalog, and I was done. I could ski a little.

I turned and drew a picture of Vancouver on the white board. I drew the mountains north of the city, trailing off into the valley. On top of them I drew stickmen on skis. I drew the Fraser River splitting off into a few channels that make up the delta. I drew fisherman reeling in giant salmon. I drew BC Place stadium so that it took up much of the city. I fit in Stanley Park using a few pen strokes for trees.

I gave a short lesson on where I was from. I told them the names of the places on the map. They asked a few questions.

It occurred to me I was making Canada look a little too perfect. Traffic on the freeway into the city was already bad enough.

I decided to make the mountains a little more menacing, so I erased the round tops with the side of my hand. I replaced them with jagged faces.

"Dirty."

"Dirty."

"Teacher dirty."

"Dirty teacher."

The girls went off.

I looked at Jake. He nodded.

Darryl came back into the class. It looked like he'd just come in from the rain.

"How's it going?" he asked

"I think they're ready," I answered.

"All right then," said Darryl. He sat down at the front.

I sat on the edge of a desk. I cleared my throat. "Okay. Let's do this."

The kids sighed and groaned. Darryl looked at them. They submitted to the inevitable. They silently nodded their heads and Jake lifted his. Joanne began her presentation on what she would do if she ran the government. She spoke as well as she wrote. I was impressed. She was a tough act to follow, but the rest did with a little prodding.

Jake sat at his desk memorizing his work. He was quiet and focused. It was almost like he was on medication. It's fair to say I liked him right away.

He did his presentation. I could tell he was nervous, but he managed reasonably well. I told him a few things he could work on so that his sentences were structured properly and so he would sound more natural.

Darryl just sat back. It was an easy first day. It felt almost too easy.

We met Yoon in the hallway and Darryl told him that I'd done a great job. He said I was a natural.

I thanked him.

"There's not a whole lot more to it than that," he said.

Yoon said he was taking us both out for dinner. He slipped Darryl a fat envelope. At the time, the largest bill the government issued was the 10,000 won note, the equivalent of 10 dollars. All the new green bills together looked like play money.

I went to gather my things from the teacher's room. Outside I heard the rumble of fighter jets. I walked over to a large window to see the show. Opening the window, I felt the heat of the night. Below, the first surge of neon mixed with the dark.

We left Ji Eun and the secretary to close the school. We took the elevator down and then we were out on the street.

There were countless little shops buzzing with activity. A number of them, mostly cell phone stores, played loud, extremely earnest sounding pop music. There were flowers and banners outside a new Chinese restaurant. A truck carrying dancing girls wearing orange skirts and long white socks stopped outside a convenience store.

Buildings, semi-built buildings with scaffolding and semi-cleared ground filled the space between the noise and neon. In most cases, the empty lots were used for parking or for dumping old office furniture and other effects.

Sometimes between buildings you could see a hint of the surrounding hills and the purple sky beyond. But, that was all.

We turned a corner and found a restaurant. Yoon ordered pajeon, or korean pancake. It is made by frying a batter of eggs and flour or rice flour along with green onions and other ingredients depending on what one wants. It can be served with beef, pork, kimchi, shellfish or other seafood.

The pancake was crispy on the outside and soft in the middle. There were pieces of squid and shrimp here and there. It was pretty tasty.

Pajeon is traditionally eaten with a rice wine called makuli and consumed on rainy days. I tried some. It was milky and sweet. It wasn't my thing.

On the table there was also a little dish called bundegi. Bundegi are silkworm larvae. I was encouraged to try one.

I put one in my mouth and instantly tried to shut the experience from my mind. It was velvety. It was the wrong kind of chewy. Time could not move fast enough. I swallowed what was in my mouth, trying to look nonchalant.

"Not bad, huh?" Darryl said as he watched to see my reaction.

"Mmmmm," I managed.

"Another?"

I shook my head. Thankfully I had a full beer to wash down what just happened in my mouth. Beer never tasted so good.

Meanwhile, Yoon talked about Korea and Korean culture. He told us how much people cared about the food they produced. He told a story about a farmer who loved his cows dearly. He said that when it came time for one particular beast to be slaughtered everyone felt terribly sad. They cried. Care was one of the reasons Korean beef tasted so good. He didn't like the beef that had started coming in from Australia.

He said, "The odds are against this place, but I love it here. I am proud to be from here. I've been to a few places. I was a bad kid. I got into fights."

I nodded. I could relate to being bad. There were a lot of stupid things I'd done that, for a long time, I let weigh on my mind. I felt I had wasted a great amount of time chasing after the wrong things.

He drank back some of the milky wine. "That's why I teach," he continued. "It's an opportunity to do something to give back. Also, in this country English is a cash cow, there is no end of money in it. In the future, I want to buy a place on a beach in Thailand. It is paradise."

By this time we had all pounded back a few beverages. I know I was feeling pretty relaxed after my first full day in the country.

Darryl made a point of saying he was really impressed by how I was with the kids. He said, "He looked good out there. He really did."

I listened to him tell a little of his story. According to him, his wife, a Canadian girl, was the best cook on earth. I didn't doubt him judging by his size. He mentioned he was always trying to get her to open a restaurant. The only problem was she had a comfortable position in town working for our competition, the Talking Moon English Academy.

I asked him how he felt about living in South Korea. He smiled. He paused. You could see him take a second to consider his answer.

"It's pretty good. I've made some great friends here," he said.

Yoon started telling us about a trip he and his girlfriend made to Canada, but I couldn't listen. My stomach wouldn't settle. I sat there having the kind of inner struggle that can only be solved by one thing.

I felt more than a little dizzy, but despite that I got up, walked casually to the tiny washroom out the back and threw up. It was a total mess. I gave myself a brief moment to let it all sink in.

I looked into the mirror while washing my hands. I put my hands to my face, hoping to wash the last few minutes away. I tried to be cool as I slipped back to in my seat.

I listened to the rest of Yoon's story. I had another pull of beer. I told him I was really looking forward to seeing the country and experiencing all it had to offer.

He looked pleased.

Darryl gave me a smile and nod, as if to say, "You'll do alright."

I stared up into the empty bottom of my pint glass.

The party broke up soon after. Yoon and I watched Darryl get into a cab and then we got into another going the opposite way. I assumed he knew where we were going.

After a turn and a little jaunt down the road, Yoon told the cabby to pull over. We hadn't gone very far. I looked at him a little confused.

"Your apartment is through there." Yoon said, gesturing at an alleyway between some buildings that looked a little like where we'd come from earlier that day.

"You sure?"

"Yeah, just go straight. See you tomorrow."

"Great. See ya."

I closed the door and shuffled over to the crosswalk. I watched the cab accelerate down the broad, modern road that separates the hulking apartment blocks. It started to rain. More cars zoomed by. I picked my spot and left the rest in the hands of the gods.

9

The next day I got up around noon. Everything is early when you don't start work until 3PM. The schedule suited me just fine. I'm not much of a morning person.

I opened my eyes. I thought about what I needed to do. I had to buy cleaning supplies. The apartment needed a thorough cleaning. I had to unpack. I had to buy some food. I had to arrange things.

I packed a few books. I had read my eyes to fatigue in university, so I was going to let up a little now. Still, it's always good to have a good book. Along with *The Razor's Edge*, I brought *Siddhartha* by Herman Hesse, *Beyond Good and Evil* by Freidrich Nietzsche and a book about Japanese colonialism. I also had a National Geographic that I grabbed from my parent's house before I left.

There wasn't much to do, so I stayed in bed and continued to read *The Razor's Edge*. I read to the bottom of a page and then dozed off.

I dreamed I was standing at the window in my school that looks north toward the downtown, the same window I watched the string of fighter jets pass the night before.

The building was on fire. It was filling with smoke and flames. I was alone somehow. I looked down at the parking lot. There was a good chance I would die if I jumped. I climbed onto the windowsill and readied myself.

Then I awoke. I opened my eyes and had a laugh. I imagined climbing down. It just wasn't possible. There was no fire escape. I'd have to slide down the bare wall and hopefully land softly on the roof of a car. There was almost no way to survive.

The shower was a new experience, as showers go. There was no bathtub. You could sit on the toilet and have the water spray down on you. Some folks I knew in Korea had apartments with extremely tiny bathrooms. Some even had their laundry machines in them to keep them company.

The water felt refreshing. Outside, the heat and humidity would be nearly unbearable - 364 more days to go.

10

I arrived to school early. I looked over some papers that Yoon prepared for me. The most important paper was my schedule.

Classes started at four and ended before ten. I would see each child two times a week for writing and presentation. Each student came on Monday and Thursday or Tuesday and Friday. I would handle 5-6 classes each day, on these days. I asked Yoon about Wednesdays. He said they would vary. He said usually there wouldn't be much to do and I could go home early.

The first block of classes I would see our youngest students. On any given day they could be the best or worst classes.

They said the funniest, most unexpected things. They told me I had a very big nose. They said I was fat. I was called dirty a number of times for a variety of different reasons.

The first lesson I taught: 'I can _____' 'you can _____' and 'he/she can _____.'

I told them I liked to play ice hockey. Some of the boys knew what that was.

Using the computer, I searched 'ice hockey' to show a picture of the game to the kids who didn't understand what I was talking about.

I clicked on a picture of a Finnish player with a bloody mouth being held back by a referee. Their eyes opened wide.

I said, "I can play ice hockey."

"Teacher, you fight?"

"No, no," I waved my hand, but that wasn't true. "Sometimes," I relented.

"Teacher dirty!"

I asked them what they could do. The default answers were, play with friends, play computer games and study.

I had them write down what the people in their family can do. I showed them the structure on the board. There were some interesting answers:

"My dog can eat teacher."

"My dog can smile."

"My dad can smoking."

"My grandfather can drink soju."

"My grandmother can make kimchi"

"My ant can sing."

"I can stand up."

"My mother can sit down."

"My mother can wash"

"My mother can go hell."

"My father can fly."

"I can do anything."

Every lesson I gave them, they gave me a little insight into their world.

In Korea, new English teachers are tested early on by wily, after-school-academy-hardened boys and girls. There are some really cheeky kids.

I didn't take anything the children did too seriously. Every now and then a young child would fall out of their chair. They would punch the kid next to them. They would put their finger up their nose. There is not much you can do.

I knew enough not to give the precocious kids an inch. I knew from my time as a student that the best way for a teacher to stop bad behavior is just to smile. Never let them see you get mad: it gives them ammunition.

The kids came in many shapes and sizes, as kids do. Some had funny English names like Doogie or Angel. Others had funny names like Wo Dong-ki.

When a new student came I was sometimes asked to give them a name. I hadn't expected that. For the first little while I gave all the boys four names, Dwight, Jim, Michael and Creed, which lead to problems later on. To keep it fresh I'd just give students a nickname at an appropriate time. A few of the names were: Meat, Polar Bear, Me Too, Hot Sauce, Lipstick, You Robot and Bamboo.

The classes I taught had odd configurations of names. Attendance might sound like:

"Jack?"

"Here."

"Jake?"

"Uhuh."

"Bubbles?"

"Yes teacher."

"Min Ji?"

"Uuun."

"Greg? Greg? Greg? "

"Haaaiiiiiiyyahhh!"

"Alrighty then. Ji Eun? Ji Eun? ...No Ji Eun? ...Okay. ...Kay. ...Mmmkay. So there's no Ji Eun then?

"NO TEACHER!!!!"

"Well, I guess she's dead."

Though, the class might have thought I was off my rocker, I thought extending uncomfortable moments of silence was a great strategy. I repeated calling out a child's name until they all became impatient. This worked extremely well with the younger ones. It was obvious little Ji Eun was absent, but this psychological trick always had the result of making young students desperate to do anything else, even schoolwork. And they paid attention. Children are unpredictable at best. In return I made sure they never knew what was coming.

I couldn't always understand what they were saying under their breath, but I could more than match them with my experience. I wasn't afraid to use everything I learned to enrage teachers against the students now under my care.

The real challenge came in the last block of classes. There might not be a sadder collection of people – Korean middle school students.

It was a test. They don't like you. They don't like themselves. They spit out one word answers like sand. I've often wondered what went on in their minds.

I remember looking out at the kids, seeing nothing. They'd avert their eyes. They'd stonewall me, not answering any question I put to them.

I guess when your life is so heavily regimented it is easy to lose hope. Most of the kids came in at 8PM having already been in school for twelve hours, minus transit and meals.

The most baffling thing was, even at such a late hour, a rare student might still be engaged. They'd answer questions without too much arm-twisting. It was like seeing a vein of gold out in the muck.

Between classes I stood by the same window as my mid-morning dream, mixing another sweet instant coffee in hot water. From beyond the buildings another string of fighter jets shot across the sky. They each let out an unnatural scream that echoed throughout the building. I wondered if I could expect the same thing each night.

I waited around after class to see if Yoon wanted to discuss anything.

"How'd everything go, Daniel?" he asked, as we walked to his office. He was carrying a tray of colored white board markers in one hand and a stack of tests in the other.

"Not bad. The kids are all okay so far."

"Good. What are you doing tonight?"

"Thought I'd go for a walk - get some stuff for my apartment."

"Have you been to Homeplus?" he asked. "There's one close by. It has everything to get you started." He pointed in the direction of the restaurant from the day before.

"I'll check it out," I said, edging my way toward the door.

"Goodnight, Daniel."

"You too."

I slipped through the glass doors, down the elevator and into the neon night. The heat hits you immediately. The aroma of charcoal and seared meat quickly follows.

I walked toward the 7/11 in search of Homeplus. I stopped at the same plastic patio furniture I'd sat at the day and smoked another cigar. I listened to the click of golf balls over head.

A group of Korean gentleman in short sleeve dress shirts and ties sat at the table beside me and I gave them a head nod and a smile.

They smoked thin cigarettes. They saw the bad boy I was pulling on and one of them made a gesture toward me. It was another in a growing list of interactions I had little grasp of. I smiled.

I got up and continuing to walk in the direction Yoon suggested. I passed by the place we ate lunch at the day before. The golf ball clicks became louder. I could hear the impact of the balls hitting screens.

I was startled to see Homeplus so soon. It wasn't far at all. It was tucked just beyond the tall buildings where I was sitting. The glowing red neon sign high above the entrance reflected off the tile in the courtyard.

It was a big box retail store with just about everything one needs to survive. It had a McDonalds. It sold liquor, wine and beer. It was open 24/7, 360 or so days a year.

Inside there was a florist immediately to the right. There was a food court to the left. I walked on to the main store.

The school gave me a number of items to get started. Along with a bed, I had a TV; a desk; a washing machine; two refrigerators; a microwave; a toaster oven; and a yellow rice

51

cooker that looked a little worse for wear. There was also a set of cutlery and a bowl.

I walked around the store trying to take in everything. There were people everywhere pushing red plastic shopping carts, clogging the main arteries of the store.

There was a lot to see. That night I walked down nearly every aisle. On the surface, it looked the same as any large grocery store I'd ever seen. However, there were a few curiosities. There was an aisle of exotic teas and honeys.

There were things in the seafood section whose English names I did not know.

There was an entire aisle devoted to ramen noodles - individual ramen, cup ramen, family size ramen and bulk ramen. There was shrimp ramen; spicy shrimp ramen; black bean ramen; spicy ramen; and there was spicier ramen. For such a space, there was very little variety.

All the workers wore red. Clerks in the meat section shouted for customers. Middle-aged ladies stocked the shelves. I had to watch out for an old man driving a tiny Zamboni that cleaned the floors. I could go on all night.

I got on an escalator to the second floor. Here I found electronics, clothes and games. There were walls of shiny flat screen TVs; there were computers; there were more aisles of vehicle and home furnishings. I could buy a rug, a desk or a chair for my office. I'd be comfortable.

I bought a solid knife and pan. I also picked up some cleaning supplies. The dish soap was easy to find. I hoped the other bottle would be bleach.

I loaded up on chicken and vegetables to make a stir-fry for dinner. I didn't buy too much. I had to walk about a half an hour back to my apartment. I hadn't yet learned to properly hail a taxi. At that point I preferred to walk with a couple bags rather than try to communicate to a cab driver where I lived.

I made my way back the way I came. People were everywhere sitting, eating, drinking and enjoying the relatively cool evening. Multitudes of children, all in a different school uniforms, moved through the streets on their way home. It was surprising to see so many were out at this hour.

I made a simple dinner when I got home. Then, I went outside and had a smoke with the old lady.

11

The next day I taught the same lessons to higher-level kids. They were a little easier to teach, but there was still a gulf between them and myself. I couldn't speak Korean and most times their English was very limited. In some cases kids were mortified to have to speak.

Teaching was a little more of a challenge than I expected, but it wasn't rocket science either. Some kids you couldn't get to sit still. Others, mostly boys, had cellphones and video games constantly on their brains.

I tried to give them something they would remember. I genuinely wanted them to learn so that we could communicate more. For such an indifferent crowd provocation was one way to get a conversation started.

I'd ask a student, "Do you like turtles?"

"Yes," they'd invariably answer (What kind of sad kid doesn't like turtles?).

"Do you like soup?"

"Yes."

"Do you like turtle soup?"

"Mmmmhh?"

That kid and the entire class would pause briefly to figure out why the phrase seemed wrong. One child would inevitably translate the English back into Korean. Some students were put off at the thought and others had a chuckle.

"Gobugi Tang?"

"Kobuki Tongue," I repeated.

"Gobugi is turtle."

"Got it."

"Tang is soup."

I'd say to the next student, "Do you like ice cream?"

"Yes."

"Do you like kimchi?"

"Yes."

"Do you like kimchi ice cream?"

Rarely would any honest student admit that combination worth recommending. Usually every student would make a face. However, sometimes one would say, "I love it" - or something to that effect.

I'd always give them a free shot at me for balance. To even it out I would point out that I have a giant nose and hairy arms.

I found that if children identify where you are going with a lesson it's over.

They don't want to be automatons, but that is how the system is set up. From the time they get up in the morning they are taught to conform, to repeat again and again. I was purposely irreverent and it seemed to work.

Even when I was killing a lesson, I'd catch a student looking at the clock. It puts you in your place. To some you are just another program – a channel that is stuck on for an hour a day every few days. I understood. They had little choice in the matter.

Having computer monitors hooked up to the Internet was a great help, though it took me a while to figure out how to make the best use of them. I'd find more than enough links to show the kids in my excessive explorations of the all mighty Internet. If they got through a lesson with a little time I would play extreme videos: parachuting, rock climbing, sharks, lions, bears etc. – there didn't seem to be any limit.

I would describe scenes as they played and have the kids recite them back. I'd write a sentence on the board. They would write the sentence. Easy stuff. I thought I had it all figured out.

Unfortunately, you can't be reliant on technology because it's too slow. There's too much waiting.

I made good use of the whiteboard. It had been a long time since I had drawn anything. When I was young I could copy images without tracing. Some drawings I did in pencil came off really well. I used to spend hours drawing, using images I found in comic books - Spiderman, X-Men, Wolverine, The Incredible Hulk the list goes on. I was a giant fan of Todd McFarlane and Jim Lee.

I began with stick figures. Stick figures work on many levels. Their charm is their simplicity. Cavemen used them to communicate.

We haven't advanced all that far. My cave was a few stories off the ground. We weren't gathered around a fire. And, there weren't long shadows stretching up the walls. Also, my writing utensil wasn't the burnt, end of a stick, but it might as well have been. Anytime I drew a head with a large nose, the kids immediately knew who it was - that was the beauty of it.

You must have some direction in each lesson. I turned everything I could into a game. I'd split them into teams – Team Strawberry and Team Kiwi. I made the kids guess what the drawing was. I gave them points. If one team started to pull away, I made the next question worth more. This way it always looked like there was a chance. If games were close, most kids would try to answer. They wanted to win. They wanted to be noticed.

One time I drew a half butterfly wing and asked a class of 4th graders what they saw. One girl guessed, "It's an elephant." Another said, "It's a dolphin." Another one, a tiny girl with an angel's face answered, "Teacher, it's a fuck you."

I didn't see *that* at all. I pretended I didn't understand. She was so adorable. How could I get mad?

Before I knew it my first week was over. Yoon waved to me saying, "Have a nice weekend, Daniel,"

I was relieved to be starting my first weekend, but I had no idea what I might do. Once again, I stepped through the glass doors. The elevator opened. I, along with a few students, got in. I looked at my reflection in the mirrored doors that were smeared with what looked to be ketchup.

Almost immediately after I crossed the intersection outside my school, I ran into a dude. I stood in front of him for a moment, lost for words.

"Hi there," I managed.

White light coming from a grocery store illuminated half of him. He was dressed casual, head to toe – faded T-shirt, torn jeans and Chucks. He was slight but tall. He looked like he'd put up a fight. He had a nest of curly red hair. It didn't look like he owned a razor. He held a dog-eared book.

Obviously he didn't fit in. Clearly, he was an English teacher. I didn't see any reason for a Caucasian dude to be in the area.

"Hey," he answered

"You're a teacher?" I asked.

He paused and then said, "Yeah, I guess."

We both stood there. People shuffled by. People on bikes swerved around us.

Being the only foreigner at my school had many advantages, but when the first weekend came I realized that I was truly on my own.

"I'm Dan."

"Lance."

"What's there to do around this place?" I asked.

He looked around and down. He squinted and scratched the back of his neck. "Not much… Anything. I'm going to have a drink with some of the other teachers. Want to come along?"

"Don't mind if I do," I said, thankful to have met someone who might act as a guide.

"I'm just headed to my apartment," he continued, "Come for a walk?"

We had a good talk. He said he was from the Midwest. He was finishing up his year soon. He had a week or so left.

He walked casually, striding over lawns and through alleyways I had yet to become acquainted with. We walked past a few bars. I noticed one named Oprah.

I figured he must've learned a thing or two about what it was like to live here. I was sure he had a few pearls of wisdom he'd be happy to pass down.

He told me we were going to Wabar. He said the place had a good stock of import beers and liquors. Along with that, it had an interesting configuration of menu items that restaurants here advertised as 'fusion' cuisine.

Lance mentioned that everyone was getting together because some fellow was going back home.

"I envy the guy," he said, as he opened the door to his apartment.

"Oh?"

His apartment was tucked away in an alley on the second floor of an older stand of units much the same as mine, a 'villa.' My apartment was on the opposite side of town.

"I've got ten more days," he sighed, pausing as if trying to remember what he'd come back for. He dropped his book on the floor and went into his bedroom.

To be polite, I closed the door after I stepped in. I took a brief survey. It was small and dank. It was littered with books and notes and bottles and cans.

He came out of the bedroom and turned out the lights. He handed me a cold beer.

"Awwright," he said, "Let's go."

"Good. Yeah."

He stared intently back at something.

"Smells like death," he apologized. "There's a squid restaurant around the corner. Mixes with the sun and…"

"Got it."

We walked back toward the downtown. There was a river to our left I hadn't noticed on the way to his apartment.

He nodded toward it, "Not much of a river…"

All the main streets that ran east west had bridges that took you over the river. Other than some shops and buildings, I didn't know what was on the other side.

"It's not a terrible place," he remarked, continuing our conversation. "It's really what you make of it. It depends on your school, obviously - and what you do with your time. I do some private lessons. I've tried to learn the language. It's just that it can get on top of you. You'll be faced with it… I'm glad I'm leaving. I wouldn't consider coming back. I honestly can't recommend it - but that's me." He added, "You might want to watch out… And cover your face."

A rusted-out blue pickup truck passed by slowly, laying down a trail of blue-gray smoke.

"What the hell?" I asked.

"Fog of death – I don't know. For mosquitoes, I think. Kills everything."

There was nothing you could do. I thought about what Yoon said earlier.

We both watched the truck as it slipped down the street and out of sight.

"Uh, well yeah," I tried to continue. "I haven't been here long. Everything seems okay. It is a little different, but my apartment is clean. School looks okay. The manager seems all right. He's about my age. Speaks English… I've got to learn the language; I've been mystified a lot lately."

"Enjoy it while it's still new." he said.

We passed the intersection where my school was located. I said I worked on the fourth floor. We stopped to get another beer before Wabar.

"Feels nice to drink a beverage while you go for a walk," I said.

"We can do what we want, until someone stops us."

12

The bar was full. Smoke filled the air. There was a large island of tables pressed together where the English teachers sat.

It was a western style bar. There were all sorts of spent bottles lining the walls. There was a wooden carving of a Native Indian wearing a feathered headdress.

All the teachers seemed to know each other. They were all joking and laughing.

The dude from Omaha offered me an open seat. I introduced myself to the others and listened as they had their turn.

I needed a drink. I sat there thinking about how I'd flag down a waitress. I thought of getting up.

Donna, a pretty girl from California sitting next to me, helped me out. She said, "See that button?" She nodded toward a little brown appendage attached to the table.

"Obviously."

"Watch."

She pressed it and a little red light came on behind the bar and there was a clear, audible, 'Bing!'

"Convenient," I said.

"That's right."

I had to be on my guard with Darryl and Yoon. I could sense right away that I'd make a few friends here. It was a tremendous relief. I couldn't believe my luck.

A waitress hurried over and I ordered a Heineken. Some of the others took the opportunity to order more. I noticed "End of the Road" by Boyz II Men playing in the background.

"Nice song, isn't it," I said to Donna.

"It is. But not here, not now," she said.

I took a second to look around. Next to her there was Crystal, a girl from England. She was sad because her pal Simon was headed home. He was seated across from her. He looked content. He got into some school to continue on as a real teacher back in Ontario. Next to him, across from me, was a big fellow named John, he wore a Denver Broncos jersey. He drank Jack Daniel's and Coke. Standing at the table was Mike, from Maryland. John, Crystal, Simon and Mike worked together. With Simon leaving there was going to be another new teacher coming soon.

Crystal said she didn't know when. She said, "You aren't going to be the newest foreigner in the 'Gok' for long."

John grinned and then threw back his tall Jack and Coke.

'Bing.'

Lance was sitting to my left chatting with a couple. I didn't yet know their names. I introduced myself apologizing for cutting in.

"Mike," said an athletic looking fellow. We shook hands.

"Nice to meet you. I'm Lindsay."

I gave her my hand.

"You're Dan?" he continued.

"Yeah, from Vancouver."

"Another Canadian."

"Canadians." Donna chimed in. "You and your flag can go and fuck off, eh."

I hoped she was joking. I wasn't so sure.

She gave me an almost serious look. It said, "Are you stupid?"

"How do you like it here?" Lindsay asked.

"It's not bad," I said. "It's different. I don't know much."

She continued, "I hated it. I hated it so much. I cried for days when I got here. It still gets on my nerves… It's different for girls. The stares - I get asked everyday by creepy old men if I'm Russian, because of my hair."

She had blonde hair. I hadn't seen any Russians. I assumed being Russian was a bad thing.

"How do you feel now?" I asked.

"You get used to it. I do yoga. I learned to give a little back, too. Now when old perverts ask if I'm from Russian I ask them if they're from China."

I tried to take it all in. Everyone seemed to be coping all right.

Some of them were going to Boryeong, a little city on the west coast, for a mud festival the next morning. They invited me along. Unfortunately, they had picked up their train tickets the week before and they didn't know if I could get a seat.

"No worries," I said.

Our table quickly filled with empty glasses. I leaned back. Another Boyz II Men track started.

"The owner has a real hard on for these guys," Simon said. It was the only thing I remember him saying.

The dude from Omaha started telling his story. He said that in the States he wrote copy for a company that imported toys from China. He said it was mind numbing – a total waste. He thought he'd try his luck elsewhere. Unfortunately, it turned out things were about the same here.

He told me he'd seen things he wished he could forget. He'd been dong-chimmed. The kids threw pencils at him. He said not long ago a little boy narrowly missed hitting him with a good size rock. Just before the boy let it go, he was casually tossing it in the air. When he realized it was a rock it was too late. The only thing preventing a terrible rock throwing injury was the boy's horrendous aim. His students constantly pulled at his arm hair. They called him fat. He tried to make light of it. He gave me a look that said, "Shit happens."

"That's why I drink," he said.

I couldn't believe it could get that bad.

He said he was off to China in a couple weeks. First he was going up to Seoul to see a friend and then he would catch the ferry from Incheon. He bobbed his head to the song playing just a little too loud in the background. "Gonna bum around. See some shit. I've got a friend there, too."

I continued to hear snippets of conversation. I told them about my school, my apartment and my boss. There was a general consensus that I'd scored a decent gig.

Donna said, "I hate you."

She had to work every second Saturday. She regretted agreeing to that the entire time she was here. She often went to her school green from Friday night.

Everyone seemed to be enjoying the start of the weekend. The RnB played on.

Later everyone went for BBQ. I was invited to come along.

Before leaving, John finished another Jack and Coke. He said, "You'll do fine. Don't worry. We're good people. Look around."

"Wish I could spark one up." I said.

"Oh yeah?" he grinned. "You don't have to worry about that around here. It's dry."

I finished my beer. We paid our bill and I got ready to walk to the restaurant. I thought it would be a little distance. However, it turns out the joint was right next door.

We sat down at a long table. I couldn't believe my luck. And then I focused on something else.

I motioned to Lance, who was sitting next to me. "Get a load of that," I said.

"Load?" he answered raising his eyebrow.

Another fellow, a Korean English teacher, said, "It's some sort of Konglish,"

"What's that?" I asked.

"Konglish," he repeated.

"I'm Dan."

"James," he said. "Nice to meet you."

I knew a little about Konglish going into South Korea from what I'd seen on the Internet before I'd come, but this was the first time I'd seen it live.

He said. "When you use Korean, everything usually ends with a vowel - McDonald'suh, Burgah Kinguh."

I looked at him.

"But not that," he continued. "I don't know what that is."

Everywhere you looked English was butchered. The examples are too long to list. Sometimes you had to shake your head.

At first you are amused and then you wonder: "Why can't they just get it right?"

You ask yourself why signs, menus and shirts are printed with such obvious errors. There are some sounds that are hard to pronounce and to the unpracticed speaker it can be a little bit of a minefield, but writing is a little different.

Across from the restaurant where we sat, a large sign on the front of a restaurant read: "Beverage and Cock."

It's a complex subject. A lot of it has to do with the effort to modernize. It's not too difficult to understand the chief motivation for the explosion in English education. People want their children to have every advantage. English sets people apart. It opens doors.

I was pretty sure that 'Cock' was short for cocktail.

13

Soju was a cheap hard alcohol sold virtually everywhere. All its victims usually emerged around midnight.

They were usually respectable looking men, mostly young, sometimes middle-aged. Most would stagger home, but others you would find abandoned on the sidewalk. Often their belongings - keys, cell phone and a half-smoked cigarette - were scattered around their bodies.

You sat at night in restaurants watching people who would surely end up there. Sometimes it was you. If you were lucky you woke up at home and can piece together some of the story. For example, how you came to be in your own bed and why there are curious drops of blood on the floor leading in all directions.

Waves of pain greet you. It's like your first hangover. You see trinkets, lighters and toy guns, that you've picked up somewhere along the way. You'll see that you forgot to close the front door.

You'll consider eating dog soup if it will make the pain stop.

We emptied our glasses to a chorus of, "One shot." and "Gumbai"

A few of us took more shots. It cut through the fat of the meat. It was industrial strength. The last thing I remember was Donna asking me to spank her ass to test its firmness.

I woke up dreading the light. The air was hot. My mouth was an ashtray. It was like something had attacked my nervous system.

I got up and hit my head on the flying plastic pig. I tripped over the bottle of water that I had placed beside my bed sometime in the night. I felt a shot of pain run down the entire length of my left side.

It was hot and it was raining. I moved to my 'office.' I sat in my underwear thankful I had an electric fan.

The night before some one had mentioned "Fan Death." I tried to find an explanation for it.

I used Google Earth to find where I was living. I saw the hill behind my house. I tried to get an idea of where I was. I needed to learn how to take a bus. I hadn't even considered using a train. I'd take my time.

It started raining harder. I was less compelled to move. I did some laundry and smoked a cigar. I thought about taking a walk down to Homeplus.

I felt I had to get out of the apartment before it was dark, before the neon cross outside my apartment lit up, but there's no going out once it begins raining.

14

The next week went by. I had nothing to do until three. I didn't really know what to do with my time. I showed up to work early a few times.

I'd welcome some of the kids who came early. I gave them a little time and attention. I treated them like children. I told them to take a hike when I needed to get some work done.

I was given no explanation of how to teach. It was a great environment to teach in. Preparation consisted of gathering board markers, a red pen and an eraser. The English lesson was usually so easy I could think of something on the fly. I was hardly overworked.

I found documents prepared by the previous teacher and tried to emulate them – I looked at the CDs for each lesson and tried to see what I could do to make the kids think and learn a little English.

One of the toughest parts is recognizing who needs help and who is being lazy. Kids who need help are amazing at covering the fact. Lazy kids drive you crazy. I was lazy. Now I've seen it from both sides. There isn't anything you can do except hope they don't turn out like you.

Early that week I went to Wabar to meet John after our classes finished. I wanted to hear about Boryeong.

He said it was a wild time.

He mentioned that the new guy was coming by for a beer. He said the new guy was all right, but he went on to say, "I don't know."

John had been around these parts for almost three years. He'd seen a few people come and go.

He said, "All I know is that he is from Australia. He's young. Anything can happen."

Mike, the fellow from Maryland who worked with John, was showing the new guy around. They walked through the door.

"Gentleman," Mike said. "This is Ian."

"Hello." I said. "Dan. I'm new, too."

"Ian."

"How are things?" I asked.

"Not bad," he said and then paused. He looked around. "It will take a while to get used to seeing garbage everywhere."

You didn't have to look too far to see he wasn't lying.

John nodded and gave a little sigh.

Ian continued, "I didn't sign on for this. My apartment's okay, I guess. The English teachers here seem nice," He looked at John. "I've started smoking just for the hell of it. When in Rome."

A few other foreigners came in. John introduced me.

"I'm Brian." One of the three said. He was a normal looking guy in cargo shorts and a T-shirt. He had on glasses and a cap.

"Ben, from Boston," another said. He was taller, skinnier, and younger than Brian.

"Colin," the third fellow said. "Brian and I are brothers."

They looked like brothers. You didn't need to look too close. I couldn't tell who was older.

They said they'd heard of me through Donna. They each ordered a beer and sat down.

Colin said that he had just signed on to teach here too. It was his second contract in Korea.

They seemed like all right people. They were off to see *Transformers* at the movie theatre. They asked me along.

"It's gonna be good. Think about it. Optimus Prime?" Ben said.

"That's all right. Gonna just stick to this," I said lifting my beer.

"Time to go," Brian added, looking at his watch.

"Hold on," Colin answered, looking at a full pint glass.

"Down it," Ian said.

"Okay," Colin replied. His face briefly straightened into a look of seriousness, as if to say, *"Who is this guy?"*

"I can down that in 3 seconds," Ian said.

"Yeah?" Colin took a healthy pull. He was obviously unimpressed.

Ben gave Brian a quick look. It didn't take much for them to come down on one side of Ian.

Ian and Mike were taking off too. They had to straighten out something about Ian's apartment with the owner of their school. They slipped down an alleyway, blending into the people and the neon.

John looked at me as if to say, "See what I mean?"

"What the fuck was that?" asked Ben.

"Douche," Colin stated.

"I can down that in 3 seconds," Brian added, laughing.

"Down it. Ben said. "Y'ever drink a beer?"

" I got it - 3 seconds," Colin said.

The boys had a laugh.

"Let's get out of here," said Colin.

"See?" John said. "He seems like a good guy. But, you have to, uh, lower your expectations here. It's a developing country. He'll learn."

I puttered around the next little while. I went to Homeplus for supplies. I wandered around for a long time. You could get lost there in the sea of people. They mostly ignored me. Sometimes they stared. Sometimes I would see my students with their families. They would wave and smile or be too embarrassed to speak.

I was pricing out hand towels in housewares when I heard "Crazy Train" by Ozzy Osbourne. The song immediately reminded me of a guy from my high school days. He was notorious for randomly roundhouse kicking people at parties. He was almost ten years older than everyone else. There is a fairly large group of people I know who experienced at least one of his kicks to the head. We always joked about him. He was lucky he never killed anyone. I looked at the cornflower blue towel in my hand and put it back on the shelf. I thumbed through different mats to place outside my bathroom. I could hear the wicked guitar licks as I strolled into the pet section with its tanks full of tiny fish.

I ran into Ian and Mike on my way back. They were outside their school's building. They were waiting for John so I hung back with them. Their school was located above the Dunkin Donuts on the main drag. There was far more traffic by their school.

I joined them for drinks at a bar by Mike's house. John showed us a video he shot of a former co-worker's apartment.

The video was taken hours after the guy left. His place looked rancid. There was garbage everywhere. You could see it stacked high and deep against walls and under furniture. John said he didn't know what was worse, the smell or the flies.

John said the guy left a few weeks before I arrived. One day he was there and the next day he was gone. A midnight run.

John said the apartment should have been condemned. Instead it was given to Ian.

John said he had to cover extra classes for a few weeks because of the hole in his school's schedule. He said that Ian was a definite step up.

We had a good laugh. Even Ian cracked a smile.

Later it occurred to me that someone like that might reflect badly on all of us. At the same time, someone *had* hired him. I didn't know the whole story and while I am usually a benefit-of-the-doubt type of guy, I couldn't help feeling glad I didn't work with any other foreigners.

I'd already begun to hear a few stories. I don't know the exact statistics, but there were more than a few foreigners living in Korea who were completely bat shit crazy.

15

Mike from Maryland told me to call him on Friday. He was going to show Ian around downtown Daegu. He said I was welcome to come.

When school ended I went home to get ready. I was excited to see something new. It wasn't long before I was back on the street, walking back toward downtown Chilgok.

The daytime heat can be so formidable that any drop in temperature is a blessing. There was a slight wind moving through the leaves of the cherry trees that line the main boulevard.

I'd pass a few convenience stores before I got to the Wabar. I'd usually cave and buy a beer for my trouble.

They were standing at the GS convenience store beside Wabar.

"Road pops?" asked Mike.

The middle of the Gok was chaos. There were too many cars trying to funnel through the narrow, brightly lit streets. People walked on the road because every inch of sidewalk was used for parking. Cars would pass by and sometimes their mirror would catch your elbow. You always had to be on guard or you could have your feet driven over. The scene reminded me of my grandpa's stories of growing up.

In a minute we were flagging down a taxi.

Mike told the driver, "Sam-duk-so-bang-so."

"What's that?" I asked.

"I asked the driver to take us to the fire station near all the bars," he answered.

The cab took off. It arrived at the tollgate.

Mike said, "This is the Gugu tunnel."

The driver tapped on the gas pedal as he drove.

"What the hell?" Ian said.

"That's just the way some people drive here," Mike answered from the front seat.

"It's pissing me off," Ian said.

The taxi raced through the tunnel and then down and around a little mountain. At the bottom it lurched to a stop at the first of a handful of traffic lights. At the next one he ran the red.

You could feel the wheels slide as we took the on-ramp onto an expressway. A car ahead of us switched lanes without signaling and our driver jacked the brakes again. This time, he even stopped a little short on Mike. I looked over at Ian. He reached for his seatbelt. I did the same.

We crossed a river. I was totally mesmerized. This was Asia. It was impossible to describe the sensation I felt as I tried to take in all the life, while also contemplating the potential end of mine.

It wasn't long before we arrived outside the fire station. There was a fire station, a church and then a 7/11 at the entrance to the city. The streets, in this part of the city, were torn up. We walked on plywood that sat atop blue cloth.

We did a tour of smaller bars Mike told us he frequented. The first one, the one that I remember, was a cozy little place with red lights. The bartenders were pretty, but the drinks were too expensive. We didn't stay long.

We went to a couple other places. Hours passed. We got split up at a place called Frog. We found each other again in Commune. Mike and Ian got a cab back leaving me there after I assured them I could find my way back.

I wanted to find the Polar Bear Bar. I remembered reading about it being in the area we were in. Somehow I found it.

I walked up the narrow stairs leading to the bar. It was quiet. Mule, the owner, was behind the bar. We talked about hockey for a bit and he said the league would be starting up soon. He kept pouring beers as we talked. It wasn't a bad place. You could buy sandwiches with Costco deli meat.

I met a couple other teachers and we went to a hookah bar around the corner. It was easy to find. It was right beside an old yellow bus that was converted into a bar.

We walked up the steep stairs. The only light came from candles set on each table. It was a respite for the senses that were spent from all the bright lights and commotion outside.

They were good people, but I never really spoke to any of them again. I only ever saw a few of them again in passing. It's just one of those things.

We said goodbye where you catch taxis in front of the fire station. Then it was just one more hurdle.

I told the first cab driver I came across "Chilgok" and "Homeplus" and "Juseyo (please)."

He looked bewildered. He put on a face like I'd disturbed him from something more important. I repeated the only two directional words I knew again, slowly. It was a no go. He'd never understand me. It simply couldn't be done.

I went to the next taxi and said the same thing twice, a little more slowly. I added, "Gugu Tunneluh."

"Gugu Tu-nurr-ahh." He motioned me in.

He steered us through the maze of exits and corridors that lead back to Chilgok. For most of the ride I wasn't totally sure if I was moving in the right direction, but we passed through the same tunnel and I relaxed a little. When we got close I said, "Homeplus?"

"Homeplus," he returned.

"Good. What are we listening to?" I said, motioning toward the radio. I got him to turn up the music a little. By his smile I could tell he didn't mind. I had a way with taxi drivers.

The fare was ridiculously inexpensive. I would celebrate my successful return with a McDonald's breakfast sandwich.

16

Outside Homeplus it was more light than dark. Upon entering the McDonald's inside the great big box, I ran into Ben and Colin talking to a cashier.

"Dannny Boooy. What's up?" said Ben. "We're having a fire under the bridge."

He wore his sunglasses in the store. "Perfect," I said.

They said Brian and another new guy were picking up some beer in the store.

"Place is wonderful, huh?" Ben said.

The place was dead quiet. It was quite a contrast to the hordes of people that were normally there. It was easily the best time to be in Homeplus.

We sat down to enjoy our morning value meals.

"They didn't have breakfast sandwiches when I first came here," he continued.

Brian and the new guy came back with a big brown bag full of beer.

"Starting a fire. Coming?" Brian asked.

"Of course," I said. I turned to the new guy and said, "I'm Dan."

"Mark, from England," he said. He gave a little wave. It looked like he had been shaken down. I noticed a little dirt on his jeans.

"When did you get in?" I asked.

"Few hours ago," he said confusedly, as if he was counting the hours in his head.

We finished up and then walked down the quiet street that leads to the river. We gathered fuel for the fire from some work sites. Every once in a while we came across a nice big pallet. I was careful not to catch my hand on any rusty nails.

There were a few others waiting under the bridge. Lance was sitting on a sheet of plywood with twins from

South Africa, a boy named Jim and a girl named Janis. They passed around a bottle of soju.

It was a beautiful time of morning, though it was an ugly time to still be awake. It was something to have a fire in Korea, at that time of day, in the middle of the city, under a bridge, next to the slow moving river.

Ben said, "Last fire, the flames were far too high."

Jim asked, "Is that the one where you burned the cat?"

"That was the first one," Brian answered. He turned to me and said, "Long story."

I didn't know it, but Jim was a wreck. Everyone called him 'Soju.' He had a reputation for getting loser pissed. He would pound back a couple bottles of the green stuff and turn into a vegetable. Sober, he was one of the kindest people.

We had the fire and finished our beers. Jim lost his shoe. He cut his foot going up the steep bank. He threw his other shoe in the river and walked back barefoot. He had the same gait as the inebriated businessmen you'd see walking home every evening. It looked like he had a brain injury.

We walked back to our homes into the sun. We must have looked like castaways. We found the space between, when everyone else was sleeping. The quiet said all that needed saying.

I got home and into bed feeling peaceful and content. It didn't last long. As I was dozing off I heard a loudspeaker cut through the calm. The sound echoed in the narrow streets. It was a man's voice announcing fresh produce for sale. He drove slowly down each street. He woke you up and left you awake until you heard the sound trail off.

17

Ben told me everyone was heading to a baseball game downtown later in the afternoon. He said Daegu had a team in the Korean Professional Baseball League called the Samsung Lions. I thought that would be just fine.

I pulled myself together and stepped outside into the searing heat. I walked down the street past restaurants, PC rooms, taekwondo studios and convenience stores. Cicadas whined in the cherry trees. Between the sidewalk and the road there were withered azaleas. Nothing could take this heat for long it seemed. Luckily, it wasn't too long of a walk.

In a peculiar place you are bound to have a few characters. Ben was unpredictable. He seemed unaffected by anything. He was honest. He could turn it on anyone. You rarely saw him without a smoke and a big brown plastic 2L bottle of Cass Red beer.

He didn't have much time left here. He was travelling on to Australia and then to Thailand.

He was sitting outside the GS on the plastic patio furniture wearing aviators and a blue Samsung Lions cap.

"What's up? I asked. I noticed a pair of crutches. "What happened?"

"Danny. You made it, "he said. He was sitting down with his leg elevated. "This," He said looking at his leg. "I don't know. Happened playing basketball this morning after you left. I was wearing flip-flops. The boys and I played a few locals at the court by my place. I wanted to win. I wasn't going to lose. Landed wrong. Shouldn't have worn flip-flops."

Before him were a few empty beer cans and a half empty pack of Marlboros. Brian and Colin were inside figuring out what else to drink.

He told me there would be quite a group. Donna and Crystal were coming. The Africans were on their way. Donna told him that John the Canadian might show up too. It was going to be a good day. We'd head out after the game and hit the town.

Brian and Colin came out with a few cold beers. We sat on the plastic patio furniture in the heat waiting for the others. The traffic was pretty intense. Beams of bright light bounced off cars streaming by.

Before long, everyone showed up. We finished our beverages and hailed down a couple taxis.

Brian spoke to our driver. He said slowly, "Citizensuhh Stadiumbb juseyoo." I stood in the background, totally bewildered. Finally, Ben showed the man his Samsung Lions cap. The driver gave a nod and, we were away.

We coasted along with the windows down. We took the route through the south side of Chilgok. It looked like the edge of town. We flew along a narrow one-way road, above a shanty town in the shadows of another new Samsung planned residential community. Brian pointed out a liquor store that carried decent whiskey. We crossed another bridge over a fair-sized river into the city.

Near the stadium the traffic seized. There was only one narrow street in front of the stadium. We got near enough and walked the rest of the way. Boston hobbled along with his bum foot.

Even though it seemed chaotic, it wasn't hard to find everyone in front of the stadium. Strangely, it didn't take long to buy tickets.

Outside the ticket counter there were vendors selling cans of cold beer. They also had fried chicken parts for sale. Brian said there were very few concessions inside the game, so it was wise to gather supplies beforehand.

We filled plastic bags with ice and then filled them with cans of beer. After that we glided past the ticket ripper, through the turnstile and up into the bleachers.

Most of the stadium seats were general admission. The stands on the third base line were packed with earnestly, enthusiastic fans - they cheered for the Samsung team with great passion.

We walked behind the giant centerfield screen and down to a quiet spot in the outfield bleachers occupied by only a few, more subdued spectators.

The players took the field under a deep blue sky.

Ben shouted to one of the outfielders on the other team, another American. He asked him to hit a home run.

Across from us, down the third base line, things were really beginning to heat up. Tiny cheerleaders danced on a stage. An announcer screamed into his microphone. The whole time those with money to waste beat blow-up Samsung-logoed plastic noisemakers.

Daegu didn't get many tourists. In Chilgok there were only English teachers. However, in the city you would also see some American soldiers. I couldn't always tell who was a soldier and who was a teacher, but most times it was relatively obvious. Anyway, you could see a few groups of young, buzzcut warriors.

We sat in our sparsely filled section of the outfield bleachers drinking and shooting the shit.

In Korea there are no peanuts or popcorn or cracker jacks. There were no hot dogs. People ate fried chicken, grilled squid and spicy ramen noodles. There was plenty of cold beer for watching the game. And, there was soju to get shitfaced.

Brian remarked that if there was a metal spike placed on the end of the plastic noise makers they might be useful to discipline unruly children. I don't think he enjoyed teaching.

Both teams came out in the 7th inning to actually stretch. It lasted nearly 15 minutes.

We made friends with the old lady who served us beer. The girls had her sit down and take a load off near the end of the game. They bought her a beer. Ben picked up her big blue plastic basket and turned to the crowd like he was going to take over.

At the end of the game we made our way through the crowd and back into taxis to take us downtown. We went from bar to bar before ending up at a place called The Crow Bar. There were lots of other young foreigners doing the same thing. It was a good enough time.

We caught a taxi back to the Gok. There, we stopped at a 7/11 for supplies.

"They wouldn't be able to handle it," Brian said. "It might look modern, but they still have a way to go. Pot won't help this place. Everybody moves too fast. It's for the damned," he added, half joking.

I thought he was wrong. "They might mellow out a little bit," I said. "They had it here before the Americans came. Maybe it would help people slow down and think."

Colin, who was silent for most the evening, shared his view. "Americans saved this place. It would just be a hole for Kim Jung Il to piss in if they hadn't stepped up. Most of the people here are oblivious. They like their soju. It allows them to continue on with their heads up their asses - we've all seen what it does…"

As he was talking he looked like he was going to walk over the hood of a car parked on the sidewalk in front of him, but then thought better of it. "They're peasants in suits," He added, and then he spat on the sidewalk.

Ben ambled down the street on his crutches. He had a cigarette in his mouth and still managed to hold a big bottle of Cass Red with two free fingers. He still had his sunglasses on even though it was past midnight.

"I can't wait to smoke," he smiled. "It's been almost a year. I'll find some in Thailand. This place is madness. We drink a lot, but you don't see us get so bad we end up sleeping between cars," He finished and then nodded toward a soju victim passed out next to a Hyundai.

"Never fails," Brian said. He shook his head looking at the poor man. "I've never seen anyone smoke a bowl and pass out in the street."

"Or get violent."

"True."

"I've smoked for years," I said. "I miss it, but I don't need it. It's everywhere back home. It's good to have a little break and clear my head, but I would like a little puff right now."

"Not with these lights," Colin said seriously. "How could you ever relax here?"

There seemed to be no end to the humanity. Cars were parked all along the sidewalks and there was garbage everywhere – wrappers and bottles and papers and cards advertising tight young ladies. People sat on picnic tables outside glowing white convenience stores, slurping ramen and downing cheap beer and soju. They smoked thin cigarettes. Some were on phones. More people stood in front of food carts dipping odeng, or fish cake, skewers, into communal spicy soy sauce bowls. Families sat in soju tents. Drunken businessmen helped each other down the street. A young couple shouted and screamed while their friends stood aside with arms crossed.

18

We arrived at Wabar. They said they had a card that allowed them to have any food item off the menu if they ordered two import beers. Ben and Brian each had a card. We ordered four beers and chose a couple plates of food – some fried chicken wings and a quesadilla.

I asked them how I went about getting a card.

Well... Here's how it goes," Ben began. "See those yellow towers? Go find mine."

From their seats, Colin and Brian eyeballed a display near the bar.

It was a wall of shelves filled with square plastic, see-through yellow towers all about 18 inches tall. There were a different amount of bottle caps in each one. I found Brian's.

Ben said to bring it over to the table. "We're going to set you up," he said, slowly getting up and taking off with the tower to find the owner of the bar.

Brian explained, "When you fill the tube with beer caps they give you a card. You keep the card forever. It's pretty handy," He took a drag of his smoke.

I nodded.

He said, "We'll get that card for you pretty quick. It goes quicker when you buy a bottle of hard stuff. Those caps take up a lot of space."

Colin laughed. He took a few pulls of his cigarette and it disappeared. He lit another and pressed the button to summon a waitress.

Ben came back with the tower. It had my name written on it.

The server came to our table with a bottle of cheap tequila and four glasses. She came back with the food we ordered.

We were the last people in the bar. I thought the night was finished.

We walked toward the GS and decided to have a final nightcap as light began to peak out from around the tall buildings.

I went inside the store to get a beer. Ben was at the counter talking to the clerk.

"This is Jun," he said to me, indicating the guy behind the counter.

"Hello," said the guy.

"Jun's cool. He's a photography student. Sometimes he drinks with us."

He was a nice fellow. He worked the night shift. He knew a little English. He knew to pop the top off your bottles. I saw him quite often.

We walked outside. The door let out a terrible ring every time a customer entered or exited. Jun must have gone mad working there.

Outside, the conversation turned to sex. They told me that barber poles, such as the one that hung from my building, didn't necessarily signify a place where you could get a hair cut. There were barber poles in and around nearly every building in Chilgok, especially in the area around Wabar. I was told you had to be careful because some places would just give you a haircut.

Ben said the barber pole operations were different from the Sexy bars. There, you had to buy an expensive fruit plate or some other menu item and then you'd have to buy a bottle of whiskey or tequila. You are expected to pour a drink for a scantily clad college student whose job is to sit and talk with patrons to stroke their egos.

"It's a giant rip off," Ben said. "First of all, what am I going to talk to her about? Chances are she doesn't understand English. Is she going to help me with my Korean? It's a little late for that. The bottles are ridiculously expensive. I'd rather bring a bottle here."

The Sexy bars were different from the Juicy bars. These bars mainly cater to U.S. military. The girls in these establishments were recruited from the Philippines to service the fighting men.

There were other places you could go too, only bigger. There are red light districts in every city. You didn't need to look too hard.

Ben said that he'd gone down to Busan with the dude from Omaha and had a good time. He said you had to keep your head on straight there or you might get in trouble with people who knew how to handle their business.

A few more foreigners came by. They sat down outside with us. I hadn't met them. They were from a school on the other side of the river. Brian and Ben knew who they were.

Jun took an opportunity when there weren't any customers to come outside have a smoke and clean up our table, which was starting to overflow with cans.

One of the guys who just showed up said to Jun, "Hey buddy, can I bum a light?"

Colin said, "His name isn't Buddy. It's Jun - I'll punch you in the fucking face." He was perfectly calm. He took a drag of his smoke.

Everyone went quiet for a moment, but when nothing happened the tension seemed to disappear.

The others didn't want anything to do with Colin. He laughed. He turned to me shaking his head, "Fucking assholes."

A couple motorbikes blazed by. They weaved dangerously. The drivers had no helmets. They rode along in t-shirts and track pants, two to a bike.

Ben stood. His glare followed the bikes down the street, "They're everywhere."

19

I met Brian outside Wabar on Thursday. A few of us were getting together to have dinner and he said he'd show me how to get there.

He told me Colin left. A few nights earlier he went back to Canada on the first flight out of dodge. Korea wouldn't have him. He couldn't get his paperwork processed because of something that happened at his first job in Seoul.

The last week or so he was waiting for word from immigration so he could make the trip to Japan to get his passport stamped. Unfortunately, he had been flagged.

Brian said about a year earlier Colin took a job near Seoul. It didn't take long to realize that the company didn't intend to honor its contract. The working hours were much longer than they let on, the pay was less than he was promised and the apartment was one of the nightmare jobs that foreign teachers tend to end up with. Any self-respecting person wouldn't stick around.

When Colin told his manager that he was done, the owner had a fit. He got the police involved. This is what kept him from teaching.

It was a shame. I hadn't really got a chance to know him. I thought he was a pretty decent guy.

Lance also vanished. He disappeared after the night under the bridge.

Mark from England took over his terrible flat. I pieced it together that the Africans and Lance worked at the same school. There were two different branches. That was the reason they knew each other. Occasionally I'd see Mark from England and the Africans walking home after work. I hadn't really even thought of Lance. I was thankful that I ran into him.

I was just getting to know Brian. Once I got past the raging alcoholism, I could see that he was a complex guy. He had a lot going for him. He graduated from one of the top schools in Canada. He knew a lot about photography. He played a little guitar.

He said he was an economic refugee. After graduating from school he had to find a way to pay off his student loans. His brother suggested teaching in Korea. He admitted that before he came he couldn't find Korea on a map.

I told him I just found out my school was closing for a week for its annual summer vacation. My boss told me he had planned a trip to Thailand.

I didn't have a plan. I was just settling in to work. I didn't need a vacation at all. I didn't have a whole lot of money. I didn't want to use half of my vacation days right away.

What could I say? I wasn't told about this vacation period when I signed on. It was a little hard to swallow. Still, I'd make the best of it.

"That's the way they are," Brian said. "They spring shit on you. No one here is organized. No one gives a shit about you."

"Where's this restaurant?" I asked.

"Down a little way."

We had to avoid a restaurant, whose owner had harassed him a few months earlier, so we ducked down a different street than I'd usually go. It was another long story.

"It's hard to keep track of all the people here I don't want to see," he said. "I ate at this guy's seafood restaurant once and he insisted I come back a week later to drink soju with him. I couldn't make it. So then, I was walking by one night and the guy came out and got in my face. I couldn't understand what he was saying, but he seemed upset. The guy cared a little too damn much. Now I have to walk this way."

"What can you do?" I said.

"He'll just have to accept that we aren't going to be best friends."

Thursday night dinners at Joe's restaurant started with Lance, Brian and Ben. I was told they found his place during the winter the year before.

From our seat at the GS25 a few nights before, you could throw an empty beer can to the restaurant.

Brian, Ben and I sat enjoying the breeze. I told Ben about my unplanned vacation.

"Don't sweat it," Brian said. "That's the way things are done here. Everyone works on a need to know basis. They need to know a lot. They don't know what's going on most of the time."

He pulled out a cigarette and stood up to take a lighter from his pant's pocket. He glared at a couple of the kids on scooters who terrorized our, relatively, peaceful evenings.

"Fear is the path to the dark side," added Ben. He passed his smoke to Brian to use as a light.

We didn't wait long before the rest of our party arrived at the GS25. Donna and Crystal came around the corner on their bikes. English Mark appeared from out of an alley in the direction of his apartment. Everyone was there. We finished our beverages and shuffled over.

I met the owner, Joe. He looked younger than his age, perhaps because he had a wide smile. I rarely saw him without it.

Other than a few key words like *maekju* (beer), soju and *juseyo*, I was pretty lost when it came to communicating. Most of the others had been here a while, but no one was close to fluent in Korean. Every transaction had the potential to be awkward and fumbling.

Teaching English in Korea changes the way people socialize. Donna laughed at me when I explained an event at my school that day because I was using my hands to help tell the story. She told me that everyone starts to use their hands more when they talk. Also, people start to talk slower.

Donna said, "When my sister visited she thought something was wrong with me. I didn't notice – you speak slower, sounding out every syllable."

"Like a retard," Brian said. "This place makes you retarded. It's an occupational hazard."

Joe's had refurbished oil drums that served as tables. There was a grill in the middle and everything else was set around it. It was ingenious, though the heat would warm your beer if you weren't careful.

We ordered big bottles of Hite, a Korean beer that's decent enough if you have no other choice. We asked for seven orders of *samgyeopsal*. Samgyeopsal means, roughly, three layers of fat. It's the same part of a pig as bacon only it is cut thicker and it isn't cured. Joe seasoned it with a secret recipe.

Before the meat arrived, a pretty young waitress set our table. There was kimchi; a spicy red pepper soup with bean sprouts; a scrambled egg soup to offset the heat; sliced raw onions in a wasabi soy vinaigrette; bowls of sliced garlic for the grill; there were dipping bowls with *ssamjang*, a fermented bean paste. Each person also received a dipping bowl with sesame oil and sea salt. And finally there was a basket of leaf lettuce and sesame leaves for wrapping everything together.

Then Joe came with a stainless steel tray loaded with meat. First, you grilled it and then cut it with scissors into bite-sized pieces. Then, you took a piece of lettuce and placed the meat on it. Next, you took a little roasted garlic or kimchi and added that to the wrap. It was a near perfect balance of salt, fat, garlic and heat. But, the dinner felt somehow incomplete if you left it at that. You needed soju, a little liquid harmony.

"But, I've got to teach tomorrow," I said.

"Tomorrow is Friday."

"Don't be a bitch."

"Everyone's doing it - even the ladies."

"I don't want to, but I will," said Donna.

"That's what she said."

"One shot," Brian said.

There is no such thing as one shot. One night of shots is usually closer.

Donna and Crystal told us that they were heading to China in a week. They were going with John. They were going to start in Beijing and then catch a train to Xi'an to see the Terra Cotta warriors.

After dinner everyone moved back to the GS for a nightcap. The girls left first. Before they left Brian called them, "Bitches on Bikes." The girls had developed a sign with their fingers making out "B.O.B." They threw it up before peddling off.

Soon after, another foreigner I hadn't met walked toward us. He was a great big fellow from Newfoundland. His hair was grey, he wore tiny glasses and he was missing a tooth. His name was Bart.

You never really know where someone comes from. The rest of us were younger. We hadn't had much time to accumulate good or bad karma. None of us were pious. We each had our share of sorted stories. Bart was definitely an outlier. He was the oldest foreign person anyone had seen in the Gok.

It was immediately clear he'd had enough of Korea and Koreans. He said he was sick of the staring. He wasn't treated with any of the reverence that the younger teachers received, and that wasn't much. He wasn't planning on staying very long. He said he'd eventually like to end up somewhere in Thailand. He wasn't headed back to where he'd come from.

The only thing I remember him telling me about his past was that he had started off as a fisherman and then he went back to school to study History when the Atlantic fishery closed.

At first I couldn't imagine him teaching children, but I think he took his job quite seriously. I think most of us did, in our own way.

Only two things suited him here. First was the food. He told me the places to go to and those to avoid. He knew all the good places.

Also, he had *the fever*. He loved Asian women. However, for what he was after Korea definitely wasn't the center of the universe. He told us about his travels.

Bart laughed when he heard the boys had told me about the not so secret sex industry in Korea. He said he'd show me a thing or two if I wanted. He was going down to Busan soon. He said he mainly went for the quality borscht found in some of the more established Russian restaurants.

That night he told me where the black market in Daegu was. He went down there for the American Marlboros. He couldn't smoke anything else.

Meanwhile, beer cans filled the table. Jun looked after us. The sun looked as if it wanted to come up and so we all decided it was time to go home.

There was only one more day of work left. Fridays were presentation days. I didn't have to any teaching. I looked forward to seeing everyone again at Wabar.

The next Wednesday I found time to get out and explore. I took the #2 Rapid bus downtown. The first thing you saw when you get off was an Outback Steakhouse. There were crowds of people coming and going. Taxis lined the streets. Buses came and went.

I found the 'black market.' It was a colorful place. It was a maze of shops, selling almost identical products. It had some stuff from home, but most of it you could get at Homeplus. I walked around the crowded booths looking at dusty, outdated bottles of Old Spice aftershave, Skippy peanut butter and Jack Daniels.

After that, I found the Kyobo department store. It had the only store in the city that carried English language books. It had a decent selection. I was pleased to see there were a number of classics. I didn't buy anything, but it was nice to know that I could.

When I left the bookstore I headed off in the opposite direction from where I came. I walked down a narrow alley lined with coffee shops and restaurants. I turned the corner where there were clothing stores and accessory shops filled with groups of young girls.

Then, I walked down a quiet street where the only items sold were power tools. The next street had only shops selling fans. Soon, I'd be into lights and light fixtures.

Around the corner there was a man, sitting in his shop, carving a beautiful wooden sign. Outside his sign was all neon.

Later, I found a Buddhist temple and I was about to take a photo of the silhouette of a small Buddha statue against the setting sun, but the batteries in my camera were dying. I managed to get a shot, but I thought I'd have to come back again.

I crossed a busy intersection and came to an old Catholic Church. The church sat up on a hill, but I hadn't seen it since tall buildings all around blocked my view.

I had to walk through a dark path and up some steep steps, in order to take it all in. There was an old man coming down. We nodded to each other.

I walked around to see if I could fit the entire building into a photograph. There was a wonderful circular stained glass window set way up so that you could barely see it.

It was quiet. I relaxed for a moment and then turned around to scout out a secluded place to relieve myself.

Around some overgrown shrubs I came across the hand of god. It was a bronze hand suspended in the air over a similarly bronzed face of, what looked to be, Jesus Christ.

The hand was muscular and covered with barbed wire. I could understand why it was left in an unattended corner of the property.

I stood there for a while trying to comprehend it. It made me think of something Brian told me. He said he went to a buffet downtown one weekend. It was another fusion place. He said he filled his plate and sat down. He was getting down on his food when he came to a twice-baked potato. He was thinking it would be *something*. It was, but in a different way.

It looked the same as back home. It had melted cheddar and mozzarella cheese on top. There were even chives. However, no one mashed the inside. It was just a hard potato with melted cheese.

At first, I thought there was a little to do besides drink. But, that little walk opened up my eyes a little. Up every dark path lay the potential for some sublime discovery. This one was pretty comic. When I got the chance I would have to show the others.

20

It was just past 2AM when I received a call from my boss.

"Hello."

"Daniel?"

"Yeah... Yoon?"

"Yes. How are you?"

"Not bad. Just relaxing," I said. I thought it was rather late for a call from the boss.

"Want to get a drink?" he asked.

"Now? Sure." I didn't see any reason not to. I didn't feel I could say no.

"I'm just about at your place now."

It was strange for him to call. Maybe he wanted to talk about something important? I was on my guard.

I went outside to meet him. A taxi pulled up shortly after and he got out. He had a smoke in his mouth. He wobbled a little as he paid the driver.

After, we walked down the street looking for a place to happen. He wanted to sing a few songs. I didn't care either way.

He asked me how I was doing. I told him I was fine. I didn't have any complaints. I liked the food. I was having a decent time teaching the kids. They seemed to like me. My apartment was nice. The walk to school wasn't too long. I was getting used to the heat.

He said, "It feels like you are out of the way in Chilgok. Maybe you'd like to move downtown. There's a little more action."

I told him that I was happy with the area. It was clean. There was enough to do. I met some other teachers from nearby. They were a good group.

We walked into a small Noraebang a few minutes from my apartment. It was a little mom and pop operation. You could hear people inside singing from out in the street. It was

93

a little louder inside. Yoon negotiated with the lady at the front. He ordered a few beers. We were lead to our room.

He said that he had to work late. After that he met a friend he hadn't seen for a long time and they lifted a few pints somewhere near Wabar.

The lady came in with two large bottles of beer and two tiny glasses. He lit up a cigarette and offered me one.

His phone rang and he excused himself. I started singing "Knocking on Heaven's Door" by Eric Clapton. Half way through the song Yoon stepped back into the room.

I finished the song well. The computer gave me a 99. It's a good song to warm up with. You can't just start with any song.

For a while we got into it. Yoon picked "Don't Go Away Mad (Just Go Away)" by Mötley Crüe. It was a little surprising to see a Korean fellow sing an old rock tune and sing it well.

It was a strange way to hang out with my boss, but we actually grew up liking the same music. He knew Ratt and Cinderella and Poison and Iron Maiden. I sang another power ballad by Skid Row. He followed with "Wind of Change" by the Scorpions. I told him when I was a kid my mom took down the hair-metal posters I put up on my wall.

As the night started to wind down he asked me if he could stay the night at my place. He told me his place was a little far away and he didn't want to wake his girlfriend.

I offered him the spare mattress, a blanket and a pillow. I said I was sorry that I couldn't offer him something more comfortable.

He said he'd be fine. He just needed a place to crash.

I slept hard. I woke up and realized my boss was sleeping on the mattress in my spare room. I was a little groggy, wondering if everything that happened wasn't just a dream.

I got up and made coffee. He woke up too, a little worse for wear. He was back talking on his phone. I got ready for work.

I told him to make himself at home. He said he ordered some soup.

Not long after there was a knock at the door. The deliveryman gave us our food. There were two bowls of soup, rice and a dish with pickled radish and kimchi.

He said the soup he ordered was called Heajunguk. The name translates roughly to, "soup that cures hangovers."

While we set up on the floor, watching CNN, letting the soup cool, Yoon taught me a few more things. He said Koreans sit on the floor more comfortably because they had gradually developed pads on the sides of their feet.

On the television there was the story of Korean missionaries being held hostage in Afghanistan. They were in the process of being set free. Two of the missionaries had been killed. Yoon said it was something that divided people here.

"These people make Korea look very foolish," he said. "Why on earth are they there? They were told not to go by the government and now *we* are paying the Taliban. We're giving them money for guns. It's so stupid. It makes us look very foolish. Christians here don't get it."

"Looks that way," I said. "I don't see any reason to go there."

"These people go to a war zone and all they bring is a book. The people there don't care. They don't want to be converted. What were they thinking?"

I thought about the hand of god and the stuffed potato.

He told me he got to shoot a rifle during his army training. Unfortunately, he said, they didn't let you shoot very many rounds.

He said he'd grown out of his uniform. He patted his belly.

"How long do you go for?" I asked.

"Everyone goes for twenty two months," he said.

"That's a bummer."

"Yeah..."

"Soup's great, eh?"

It was moderately spicy. Yoon told me that it was made from ox blood. Inside the bowl I could see meat, bone and some leafy vegetables.

"What's this?" I said, enquiring about the odd shaped bone. It took up a lot of space in the bowl.

"Spine."

I pulled it out of the bowl to take a better look. "So it is," I answered.

"This soup has been eaten for thousands of years," he said. "I have it whenever I have a hangover."

After eating, we walked to school.

I asked him about the dents in my front door.

He said the teacher that I replaced knocked up a local girl. He said there was a reason he was marrying a Canadian.

Food for thought, I thought.

We taught our classes. The whole day Yoon was dragging his ass. I didn't feel much different than usual.

After class he pulled me aside to show me pictures of his BMX. He listed the different things he'd done to improve it. All I could think about was meeting the others for a cold beer.

Often he told me about some new technology he was using: music players, phones, video games, everything little, expensive and portable. He was passionate about his technology.

One of his hobbies was playing with remote-navigated gliders. He showed me videos on YouTube from time to time. He had a video of him throwing the glider he built. He showed it to me on his phone.

I tried to act interested. He'd end up trying to get me to buy a BMX, or an expensive phone. I just wasn't interested. However, at the same time, I didn't want to offend him by telling him the truth. I just nodded and told him I'd think about it.

The phone rang. It was one of the mothers. I edged toward the door. He held the receiver and said, "Good night, Daniel."

Minutes later, I met Brian at Wabar. We worked on filling my tower. I was surprised to see it nearly full. It didn't look like it would be long before I had a card. Brian told me that he and Ben were filling it up. I saw, along with all the beer caps, there were a number of larger caps from whiskey and tequila bottles I didn't remember being a part of.

I told him about the night before with my boss singing old metal tunes. I told him we watched CNN in the morning eating takeout soup on my floor.

"He stayed the night at your place?"

"Yeah... What can I say?"

You could always count on Brian for a drink and good conversation. Unfortunately, he had a terrible job. Everyday, he complained about his boss's idiosyncrasies. He told me how the guy made everyone wait after work to take the elevator down together.

"He's a fucking control freak. Almost everyday he throws a tantrum over something insignificant. I've got to get away."

He asked me if I wanted to go up to Seoul during Chuseok, Korea's Thanksgiving. He said he wanted to buy a new camera. He'd been waiting to buy one all year. After that we could go have a good time.

He said, "We'll get a hotel room and some whiskey and see some of the town. I am sure Ben will come."

He told me that since his brother wasn't going to be around his plan for the rest of his contract was to lower his head and work on his photography.

We drank our beer and went outside. We didn't get far. We stopped immediately in front of a GS25. While we thought of something to do we got another beer. It was cheaper if you bought it at the GS. It was late August. It was a pleasant evening.

"It's like the 50's here." Brian said. "It's developing, but so rapidly. People just can't adapt that quickly... I mean, why do they allow cars to park on the sidewalk? People *have* to walk down the middle of the goddamn street."

"It is different," I said. "But, you can sit outside and finish your beer without being hassled by the police."

"The RCMP get an aching hard-on when they see anyone enjoying a beer in public."

"I've never seen anything too violent happen here. It's not like in Vancouver or Toronto where you have to worry about guns."

Brian said. "One time outside of Joe's I saw a real brawl – some real Bruce Lee shit. Ben and I were eating dinner outside when two groups of people just went off. It started in the pajeon restaurant and spilled out onto the street. A few guys were covered in blood. They ripped off one guy's clothes. We ordered a couple beers while we watched."

"Savage," I said.

He continued, "It isn't as bad as the United States, or even Canada, but it's here. It's not the peaceful place many would have you believe. They don't have guns here, thankfully. Before I came here I was living with my brother in Montreal. I was in Dawson College when that guy walked in and shot up the place. That was the scariest day of my life. All you could hear were screams. I booked it. I got out of there. My dad called me because he knew that's where I was going to be. He saw it on the news. Fucking horrible. Usually the only thing we really have to worry about here is being dong-chimmed, though there have been a few times I thought I might have to fight."

"Fucked up," I said. "I've never felt threatened."

"You haven't been here long,"

"There does seem to be something below the surface. There's a lot of tension. I can't put my finger on it. Look at how much people drink. And, there are a lot of suicides – the place is number one in the world."

Brian said, "In Daejeon, my first year, a student came in late. She said her mom couldn't get her car out of the parking lot because a girl jumped from the top of one of the apartments. I wondered why she'd bother coming to class." He paused. "I've encountered enough crazy people here. There are few good one's, but I could never really think of staying."

"Yeah, there are a few good ones. My boss seems to be," I said.

"I can't believe you sang Quiet Riot... I don't want to talk about my boss. He's a cheap prick. He isn't in the business to educate kids. He sees only the dollar signs. He was a used car salesman before he bought the franchise. Says it all."

No one bothered us as we sat enjoying our beer. For most it would be too much of a bother to communicate. Few people could speak English. So we were, for the most part, treated like we weren't there. We'd get stared at from time to time. Occasionally someone might even say something other than, 'hello.'

There were rare times when people would ask where we were from. Some wanted to know what we were doing. There wasn't much more to most conversations.

This Thursday there wasn't a dinner at Joe's. Ben was having dinner with his school. His time was almost up. Lance was couchsurfing somewhere in China. Donna, Crystal and John were also in China, somewhere between X'ian and Beijing. I was a day away from my first week of vacation in Asia.

"Any plans yet?" Brian asked.

"Nothing," I said. "I had a great time before coming over. I haven't been here long enough to take time off. I'll head to Busan for a couple days, I think. We're going up to Seoul just after that, so it makes sense."

"There are a few decent bars by Haeundae Beach," he said. "There's a big fish market down there. It's interesting enough. There's the UN cemetery,"

"We'll see," I said, shrugging my shoulders.

We decided to play some pool. We tried a few places. At first glance, it looked like there were quite a lot of tables. It's just that most didn't have pockets. These tables were for a popular game called danggu. Up to 4 players could play at a time. They each had a ball. Brian said he played before, but couldn't remember the rules.

In Korea, pool was for girls. I rarely saw men playing it. Men played danggu. They only played pool if they were out with their girlfriends.

Brian said, "What's the matter? They're too good for pockets?"

We managed to find a table in a place above a restaurant called Beer Kaiser. The owner welcomed us in. Although it was full of men smoking and playing the game without pockets, there was an open table in the corner. It was relatively quiet. It was bright. It looked a little lived in. It smelled of smoke and mediocrity.

We played the rest of the night. Some games were good and quick. Some were the opposite. We noticed the table had a slight break to it. The balls curved slightly more as they slowed.

Later, the owner of the place stepped out while we were playing and came back with a couple cans of beer. He placed them on our table.

"Service," he stated.

"Cumsumneeda," we both said.

It was about 2AM when we finally put a stop to it. We had a chat with him before we left. He told us his name - Mr. Kim. We told him ours. He watched TV and didn't mind if we stayed. The place was chill. We told him we'd come back.

21

The Friday before my vacation was a breeze. I wished Yoon well on his vacation. After that I headed to the bar.

I had a few beers while waiting for the others to arrive. I recognized a couple teachers from another school. I knew one of them from before. His name was Dave. He was a young guy from Ontario. He was a nice enough.

The other guy was new. His name was Greg, from Australia. He looked to be in his 40s. He said he worked in finance before coming to Korea. Also, he said he taught a little while in Thailand. He told us a little about teaching there and picking up hookers on the beach.

I gathered up my bottle caps for my yellow tower. I went to the display to get it and noticed it was full.

Greg asked me what it was about. I explained that I was finished filling it, so I was going to give it to the guy behind the counter. After that I would receive a discount card.

"How long did it take to fill that thing? Must have been a long time," Greg said.

"About a month," I told him.

He smiled. He looked a little surprised. He probably thought I was lying. I could hardly believe it was already full.

"Everyone fills the tower for you then?"

" I'm not stopping them."

"How do I get one?" he asked.

"Find a full one and put your name on it."

I got up with my tower and took it to the bar. A pretty, young waitress took care of the rest. I sat back down and finished my beer. A few moments later she brought me the card. I gave Greg my tower and he started collecting. Dave did too.

Later, Brian told me he saw the pair collecting bottle caps from other tables. That was taking it a little too far. A few weeks later the owner put an end to giving cards to foreigners after the two tried to lift a few caps off his table. I felt it was my fault.

A few more teachers rolled in. Ian came in with Mike from Maryland. Mark from England made an appearance. He always wore funny t-shirts. He had on one with an Adidas logo that said, 'Adios.' Bart brought a new fellow, also named Greg. He was from Ontario. I thought he was a nice enough guy, too.

Brian and Ben came in later. Brian said he'd picked up some whiskey.

Greg from Australia told us about shooting kangaroos. He said that in parts of Australia they were seen as a nuisance. It was okay to shoot them. He said a few years earlier a friend took him out one afternoon. He spotted a large male and pulled the trigger. He saw the animal go down. When he got over it he saw the animal was crying. He shot its balls off. He said it was a terrible mess. He could never forget the look in its eyes.

Things were mostly mellow. But, the night escalated pretty quickly. Bart was wise enough to leave before the cheap hard liquor arrived.

We bought a bottle of Jose Cuervo and quickly finished it. We bought another. We were going to buy another, but the bartender shut us down. It was the first time anyone remembered being cut off.

We moved the party outside. Ben took it pretty well, but Brian raged. I convinced him to sit with us outside at the GS. I went in and bought a few Heinekens.

"I'm fucking speechless," he said. "It's racist... Fucking discrimination... I can't stand this shit much longer."

"Good thing you're sitting," Ben pointed out.

Meanwhile, Mark from England was totally annihilated. He had a half empty bottle of soju in his hand. He started saying things that didn't make sense. He held up random people on the street asking them, "Who's your favorite cracker?"

I was trying to keep things from going completely sideways. Then Greg from Ontario said he didn't know how to get home. We asked him where he thought he was staying, but he couldn't seem to make sense of things.

It was totally understandable. He was new. He told us a few places he remembered, so we could help him get back.

I told him I thought I knew where he had to go. Most of us lived in the same general area, so it wasn't that hard. It was the least I could do. I was new once.

He said, "You aren't telling the truth. I don't believe you."

"Why would I lie?" I asked him.

This went back and forth. I told him if he didn't want my help he could leave. I shook my head. You can't help some people. We just drank two bottles of tequila together. Ian told Greg I wasn't playing around. Ian knew I had no reason to lie. Why would I want to fuck with a new guy?

Greg ended up getting in a cab with Brian and Ben, who was still hobbling around.

Immediately after they left it started to rain. It came down so hard it bounced off the ground. I considered gathering two of everything.

After it started to rain, it was next to impossible to find a taxi in the Gok. We made our way to Homeplus because there always seemed to be a cab or two there.

It was quiet inside the great big box. Ian and I went to the McDonalds. We left Mark looking at discount jeans near the front entrance.

We were sitting, discussing the night, when he reappeared, followed closely by two security guards. He was stripped to his underwear. He was holding his jeans. He wasn't wearing a shirt. He was soaked to the bone. He stood in front of us with a blank stare.

"It's really coming down outside," he said. "Think I'll just stay here."

103

We got him out of there. He was totally incoherent in the taxi. I didn't remember where he lived exactly, so I just threw him in my spare room.

When he woke he said couldn't remember anything after the poor kangaroo lost its balls. He asked me if I knew where his t-shirt was. I told him about Homeplus. He looked a little embarrassed. I told him it was okay. It happens. That's drinking.

It was still raining hard outside. We had a smoke. He laughed a little when I told him more about the night before.

"You've got a nice view here," he said, flicking the ash off his smoke out my window. Rain was dripping off a mess of wires that'd mystify the most serene electrician. Above that stood the bright orange cross.

"Lots of those 'round here," he said.

I gave him a shirt and an umbrella for the walk across town. He quietly slipped out the door and down the street.

22

After Mark left, I tried to put together an outline of things to do in Busan.

It had a few famous beaches. The most popular of those is called Haeundae. An image search on Google nearly put me off. There were so many people sitting under yellow and blue tents I wondered if it would be too much.

I relaxed the rest of the day. It made little sense to step into the monsoon outside. It was pleasant to just lounge, listening to the rain.

The next day I woke up, made a nice breakfast and set off a little before noon. Outside it was bright and almost fresh. There were no clouds. I caught a bus to Daegu Station. From here you could only catch a local train, but I didn't know that. If you wanted to ride the KTX, Korea's Bullet Train, you had to go to Dongdaegu Station. I didn't think there could be much of a time difference and I wasn't in a rush, so I wasn't too upset about having to take the slow train. Other than the Skytrain in Vancouver, this was the first train I had ever taken.

The ride down was extremely slow. It stopped at every station. A few Seoul bound KTX rocketed by. When we got going, I followed the action on the river. Some folks stood on the shore casting their lines. Now and then I'd see a crane creeping in the shallow water. In the distance there were giant green nets of golf ranges. There were colorful temples with red, blue and green lanterns. In each town there were the same tall concrete apartment buildings towering over everything. Beyond there were quiet mountains.

It was still bright and sunny as the train approached the coast. A breeze pushed around a few bands of cloud. As the train entered Busan, buildings and streets began to compound. I tried to follow everything. I didn't know when the end of the line was going to come. I listened for the announcement.

My body tensed a little. I had no time constraints. I didn't have to worry about anyone else's plans. I was completely free. On the other hand, I didn't have anyone to share the trip with. Everything balances out.

As the train approached the station I saw a sea of boxcars lined up in the port. I caught glimpses of the actual sea beyond, between a mass of glistening red, blue, and green containers.

The train squealed along. Everyone shuffled and stretched as they do when a train nears a major station.

Finally the train reached the end of the line and I got off and made my way into the station. I wasn't carrying much. I was traveling light. I had a lot of ground to cover. I bought a coffee and a donut and sat down outside the station, in the giant courtyard. There was no use rushing. I kept my eye out for buses. I knew I had to take the #1002 to get where I wanted to go.

It was a quiet bus ride. I looked out at the city. There were more hills in Busan than I expected. The buildings all had the same slightly weathered look as those in Daegu.

I hit the exit button when I saw a sign for the UN cemetery. I got off and followed the signs. It was only about 15 minutes from the main road. Next to it, to the south, stand two hulking concrete buildings that house the Busan Cultural Hall and the Busan National Museum.

The land for the cemetery was donated by the Korean government in appreciation of the lives given by UN soldiers. It's a small, but significant piece of land in the middle of the city.

I walked around looking at the all the gravestones. I was surprised to see just how many countries made up the UN forces. There were remains of men from Australia, Canada, France, the Netherlands, Australia, Norway, South Korea, South Africa, Turkey, the United Kingdom, and the United States of America. The United States lost by far the most of any outside nation.

On the walk out I was greeted by a group of old men. One of the old fellows asked where I came from. I told him. As I walked on I heard his friends repeat with hoarse, throaty voices, "Canadahh."

I wonder how old those fellows were during the war. Some were definitely old enough to remember. That generation is slowly fading away.

The sound of traffic took over the further I walked from the cemetery. The sun had already begun to set. I caught a bus to Haeundae.

I was lost in thought, looking out at the passing city. People and shops passed in and out of the shadows and the light. I kept my eye out for landmarks and interesting places. As I said, it looked very similar to Daegu, but every now and then I'd get a little view of the ocean.

The bus passed through an area with narrow streets filled with people. I couldn't see any sign and I didn't hear anything in the bus, but I thought it was probably the area near the beach. Still, I sat waiting patiently.

The bus wound up a hill away from the lights and I thought I better get off. I picked a spot at the top where a few people were exiting. They quickly evaporated into the darkness in different directions and I was quickly left all alone.

I was close. I walked back down the street looking for a path that would take me toward the sea, however there were trees and buildings in the way. I turned a corner and I could see more lights. I bought a beer and wondered where I was.

I decided to keep following the same path and suddenly, there were people - people everywhere. There were cars moving bumper to bumper down narrow streets. There were hotels, restaurants and convenience stores. Further down I could see giant hotels, and past that I could see the lights of the massive Gwangali Bridge.

I sat on the sea wall, watching waves crash. The waves drowned out almost every sound. It was the freshest air I had breathed in a long while.

Three Korean fellows sat down next to me. One of them could speak a modest amount of English. He was an artist from Seoul. I told him I was an English teacher.

"Where are you from?" he asked.

"Vancouver, Canada," I replied.

"Very big mountains,"

"There are."

"Do you know Korea's famous mountain?"

"I'll have to find out," I said.

We ended up sitting there enjoying a couple beers. His friends went to a store and brought back squid jerky, sausages and assorted cheeses. I'd never been drawn to the squid, but how could I turn it down?

After a while, I felt the urge to move on. I said, "See you later."

They told me they wanted me to come to a club. I thought about going, but I had to be on my way.

I walked down the strip that fronts the beach. I took a few pictures. I looked into a convenience store to see what kind of alcohol I could find. There was a giant preserved sea turtle hanging on the wall. You never know what you'll find.

Before I left, Ben told me to find a place called U2 Club. I didn't bother looking up where it was. I found it almost immediately. The bar was down steep stairs. At the top I listened for life. It sounded like there were only a few people, so I decided to keep on wandering.

At the far end of the beach, it was mostly the same. There were lots of couples minding their own business. There were groups of people. There were freaks like me. Across the street I saw the burnt ruins of a McDonalds. Yellow tape surrounded it. Further down there were more franchise restaurants and narrow alleyways I didn't much care to explore. I looked for a Frisbee in a number of little shops, but there weren't any. I could've bought fireworks at nearly all of them. I won a tiny seashell key ring throwing darts at balloons. I looked at the tiny painted shell and put it in my pocket. I walked by a few more stalls, moving further down the road until I could only faintly hear the sound of the sea and it felt like time for another drink.

I wandered back down to the beach. I sat down on the boardwalk. Young folks shot fireworks up into the black leaving light grey smoke blossoms. Meanwhile a group of old folks made their way down the silvery sand gathering the day's rubbish.

There wasn't much left to see so I returned to U2. From the top I could hear a hum coming from below.

It was mostly English teaching folk - lots of young foreigners and a sprinkling of Koreans. An expat band was up on stage. I got in line to order a drink. Next to me was a teacher from Abbotsford, the town across from where I'd grown up. He said he was teaching English at a church. I thought it was fitting considering how many churches there were in Abbotsford. He introduced me to some of his friends. We had more drinks. The band played a few more songs.

Later, a DJ took over. I started dancing with a pretty girl in a red dress. This was the exotic Asia I had come to see. It lasted less than a song. The lead singer of the band cut in. I don't think they were together, but I was alone and he had a band. I had another drink and a shot of tequila.

There was a fellow standing at the bar.

"Quite a nice place," I said.

"Oh yes, zis is one of zee best," he answered.

He said he was from Germany. He worked as an engineer at a shipyard. He said he was staying at one of the fancier hotels nearby.

I told him I was a teacher from Canada living in Daegu. I told him it was my first time in Busan.

He told me about a few places to see – the fish market and a lighthouse on the other side of town. He said there was

109

a decent businessmen's hotel back by the train station. He wrote down the name for me to give to a cab driver.

He asked me if I wanted to see another club he knew. We finished our drinks and walked across the street and back downstairs into a space with pulsing black lights.

It was dead. The music was loud and I felt old. There wasn't anything to do except empty my glowing beverage. After that, I thanked the fellow and made my way back out into the night.

There was nothing left to do. Outside the club the rain was coming down hard. I had no umbrella, so I waited on the corner until a cab stopped in front of the club. I told the driver to take me to Busan Station.

It was quiet out in the streets. I wasn't sure of the time. It didn't matter. It didn't take long to arrive.

The hotel was right next to the station. The night attendant said there was a room. He asked for a scan of my passport. I'd have to behave. I picked up snacks for the morning at the GS25 next door. I rode an elevator up to my room on the 8th floor.

Once I was inside I looked out the window. Looking down I saw lights around the station. The rain came down hard. A few people moved quickly through the square.

I paced around. I saw a fat cockroach in the bathroom. I found a magazine to kill it with, but when I went back in the bathroom it was gone. I wondered how I would sleep.

I sat on the bed and flipped through the channels. There was old soft-core porn on one of the lower numbers. An old man was raping a young woman. On the next channel an old man yelled at me and then he stuffed some meat into his mouth. Not long after I must have drifted off.

The next morning I gathered my things and checked out. Outside, it was bright and clear. I walked toward the fish market through strange, sour alleyways and backstreets.

I made my way west for about a half hour. I saw a sign for the ferry to Japan. I considered going. I thought about the poor timing of my vacation.

I saw men fishing just off the street. The water is twenty feet or so below where they were standing. A constant stream of automobiles motored by twenty feet from them. I peered over a railing at the water below. There was all manner of floating debris slowly disintegrating against the concrete shore.

I wondered if they caught anything. I wondered what you'd catch. I wondered what you'd do with it. Next to them I saw a few other old men sleeping on cardboard on the ground.

Just before the fish market the buildings stop obscuring everything and the scene unfolds. There were boats of all shapes and sizes. There were freighters that sail the world and tiny aluminum skiffs that I wouldn't feel comfortable in. There were new boats and old boats. They come in every color from white to rust. There were ferries that take people all over the region. There were fishing boats. There were boats for reasons I'll never know. They motor back and forth through the gentle waves of the harbor.

The west side of Busan is built up over the water. It seems nothing natural meets the sea.

This part of Busan has a character all its own. There was a little more diversity here than in Daegu. Instead of soldiers you'd also see crusty sailor types, the crews of all the ships that came and went.

It's been a dream of mine to catch a ship from Asia back to Canada. The idea first occurred to me when I saw Vancouver from the bottom deck of a BC ferry on a rainy night returning from Nanaimo. I was in my early twenties.

I was with my family. We were returning from my uncle's funeral. I never knew him well. He was married to my dad's oldest sister.

111

My cousin, my sister and I went below to the car deck and polished off a few bottles of wine. Our families were all probably having coffee. I think my brother was upstairs studying for school.

There had been an advisory warning of rough seas. I hoped there would be. The wine tasted right. It was clean and dry and gave me courage. We stood watching the large waves break over and over. White caps stretched down the straight. Right below, the sea was deep black and formidable.

When my cousin left I fired up a joint. My sister and I passed it back and forth.

We stood out a while longer and slowly the city's skyline emerged from behind the horizon. I had never seen Vancouver from that perspective. It gave me an inkling of what it might feel like coming from further away.

To get to the fish market I had to go under a busy street. There were random stores; there was a GS; there was a bakery; and, there were a number of clothing stores carrying sweaters and blouses that looked like they'd been on sale since Ben Johnson ran in Seoul. On the other side I found a map. I was moving in the right direction.

The fish market was something to behold. There were more species of sea life in and around it than I could ever name. I bet Marine Biologists would have trouble identifying some of the creatures brought up from the deep. I walked around taking pictures of fishmongers preparing their fare. The old ladies doing prep work seemed happy in their rubbers. You could hear their cackles over everything.

I stepped outside, toward the concrete shore. Sea gulls flew everywhere. There were squid laid out in an area the size of my old high school gym. I stopped to take a photo of them.

The street in front of the main market was hopping. Steam rises throughout the narrow crowded avenue. Everywhere there were ladies hawking fish. At any given time you can see fish being gutted. Under the makeshift, multicolored canopies you see ladies frying fish; others make soup; more still try to get people passing through to stop and eat.

I sat down at a restuarant and ordered some sashimi. It was served with a number of side dishes. There was white kimchi and a red, spicy fish head soup.

Busan had a few things I didn't expect. It had palm trees. The coast is nothing to jump up and down about, but one can sit out and listen to the waves and imagine where they originate. The city itself is divided by hills. Bridges and overpasses do their best to erase the separation. I never got to climb up a hill to get a better sense of it. I knew I would come back. There was a lot left to explore.

I decided to take a train back to Daegu. It wasn't going to get dark for a while, but I didn't want to wander around any longer. I caught the KTX back. It took only 40 minutes or so to reach Dongdaegu Station. From there it was just a short taxi back to the Gok.

23

It was quiet when I got back to town. I thought I'd make a detour toward Wabar to see if anyone was around. On my way I saw a new batting cage in the center of town. I had passed the same way many times; there was nothing when I left for Busan, but now it was a fully functioning family entertainment center.

It had five stalls. Each stall was a different speed ranging from 110 to 140KM per hour. In front of the batting cage there was a machine with a pad where you could test the power of your punch; there was another game with a soccer ball attached to a lever that you kick, but it looks like you can also break your shin on it; there was also a game with two basketball hoops that you can find just about anywhere; finally, off to the side, there were a few trampolines. There were a few people around shooting hoops. There was a guy hitting balls in the stall to the far right. How could I not take a turn?

I had to take a few practice swings to remember what it felt like. My body felt horrible. It creaked. It had been a long time since I'd made a swinging motion with a bat. I hadn't done anything physical since arriving just under two months earlier, unless you count pouring pitchers and turning meat on an open flame.

Growing up I was a decent ball player. It was easy then, but those days were gone. I had braces on my teeth then and a mullet - like a young Don Mattingly. I took a few more swings trying to focus on the feel of the bat head. I popped some change into the meter and had a go.

I only managed to connect with a handful of balls. My hands stung from all the balls I hit off-center. It was pitiful.

It was a definite shot to my ego, especially when I noticed that a few children had stopped to watch. They laughed. They covered their mouths with one hand and pointed with the other. Cruel.

I wasted away the next few days exploring the area around my house. It was good to get out and see a little more of the area under my nose. There were schools. Many schools. There were an enormous amount of restaurants. Some had curious signs. A few were written in English. One menu advertised: 'Glutinosity Fried Pork.'

There were enough bars within a ten minute walk of my house I could have picked a new one each day for about a month and never seen the same place twice. If I walked another ten minutes I would be set for the entire year.

I decided to see a little nature. I lived at the foot of a mountain named Hamjisan. The start of the trail was a ten-minute walk from my front door. On the street leading to the entrance there were lots of people selling outdoor supplies I'd never need. I avoided looking at any of the fancy gadgets they were selling and shuffled past a few old folks in technical mountaineering gear. There were actually quite a lot of people as you got going.

I made a wide birth around a stand selling roasted bundegi. The strong smell wafts directly into the GS25 right next to it. I felt sorry for the person working there. For me, it was a few seconds of horror. I don't know how one could take something like that for hours. Some people don't mind it. When I saw the grease-stained roasting cauldron I walked faster.

I walked up some steps to a reservoir. You walk along its bank until you reach the trailhead. The entire trail there were speakers set above your head on posts. The music that came out of them sounded something like the soft hits of the Korean 70's.

At the end of the trail there was an outdoor gym. There were people working out; some were using weights; others were stretching; still more were using weighted hula-hoops.

I kept moving, turning up another trail. It looked as if it had been used for ages. There were steps carved into the red soil. In places, the rock was worn from all the traffic.

After twenty minutes I came to a plateau where the path splits in two. There was another smaller outdoor gym. There were a few people here and there. An old guy walked around with his hands behind his back, pressing his chest forward. At the entrance to each trail there were Janseoung, or Korean totem poles, made from pine trees.

I chose to go up the trail to the right because it looked to offer a view of Chilgok. I would check the second path another time. There was a steady trickle of people, all wearing the newest technical mountaineering gear. Some used trekking poles. I was wearing flip-flops.

I kept on moving up the trail. It wasn't too difficult. There were a couple times when it got steep and I had to use my hands. There were no tall trees, only short, twisted pines. The wind made whistling sounds. There was bush on either side of the trail and it looked like it fell off steeply in a few places.

It took about 45 minutes to reach the top. There were some nice rocks to sit on next to a cell phone tower. I could see down into Daegu. Much of the city was covered in a thick haze. I could see into Chilgok on the otherside. It was much clearer, but it was also closer. I couldn't see Wabar or my school. The tall apartment buildings blocked them. From the sky beyond, a string of fighter jets roared toward the airport. They came from out of the clouds to the northeast of Chilgok.

Further, down a little way on the other side of the peak I noticed a sign saying that the area was a fortress during the Three Kingdoms period that lasted from 57BC to 668AD. Judging by how far you can see in either direction, it was the perfect spot.

I made my way up the second peak. There was a helicopter pad on top of it and an even better view into everything. There was a trench built all around it and I followed it down the ridge, stepping over pampas grass and light pink cosmos. Every so often you'd see a nook where they set up mortars during the Korean War. Here and there, in the open and in the shade of the thick forest of pine trees I saw tiny, well maintained burial mounds. I didn't know how old they were.

At the end of the ridge there was a friendly old guy. He asked me what I was doing in Korea. I told him I was a teacher. I told him where I was from. There was always difficulty communicating, but I was adjusting. I'd learned a little Korean.

He offered me a big red apple.

I couldn't say no.

I bit into it.

"Sa Gwa, Korea famous apple," he said.

"Delicious."

"Delicious," he repeated.

I shook my head. I'd never had a better apple.

"Delicious Korea - maasheesaeyo."

"Maashesaeyo," I said.

He smiled.

I got up and gave the man a little bow saying thank you and cumsumneeda. I set off down the quiet trail. Near the end there was a tiny Buddhist temple and after that there was the dusty dirty city.

It was only a slight change in perspective, but it was somehow what I needed.

At that time I was having a hard time falling asleep. I've never slept well in the summer. I'd stay up reading or surfing the Internet until it was beginning to get light out. It was usually quiet, but not always.

One night I heard a scream outside of my apartment that gave me chills. I looked out my window and saw a group walking from one of the bars nearby.

A young woman was fighting her boyfriend. For a few moments, it was intense. She took a swing at him and he didn't hold back on her. She fell to the ground and he held her down.

I felt I should do something. I wasn't comfortable with the way the guy took control of the lady. When she tried to get up, he put her in a headlock and didn't look as if he would let go. A few people, I took to be their friends, stood there doing nothing. I looked on waiting for something to happen.

What could I do? Domestic disputes like that are hard to step in the middle of. It wasn't any of my business. However, the scream reminded me of a murder that happened near Vancouver a few years earlier. When investigators came around people reported that they had heard a woman screaming, but they didn't do anything at the time. They went back to sleep when the screaming stopped.

The situation outside seemed to calm down. I stayed up a little while after thinking about what happened.

I met Brian and Ben at Wabar later that week. I told them about what I'd seen.

"You don't want to hurt someone and have to deal with the Korean justice system, Ben said. "The girl is liable to side with the man beating her. If you try to be a hero, anything can happen."

"I've seen more domestic violence in two years in Korea than I saw my entire life in Canada," Brian said. "The couple living above me constantly fight - I can hear him beat her. One time I had to call the cops. They actually came and put an end to it."

"Calling the cops seems to be the move," I said.

I mentioned the batting cages. Ben gave me a nod. He said he took some cuts before work when he had time. Brian said he'd also put in some time there.

It was a real nice addition to the area. We finished off the night taking turns feeding coins into the machine. Every now and then I caught one pure.

The weekend came and went. Before long it was Thursday and I was sitting at the GS near Joe's having a beverage with the boys. Brian said Donna, Crystal and John were back from China and they were all going to be there.

That night it was a little cooler, so we moved inside. There were original movie posters, written in Hangul script, from *Star Wars* and *Enter the Dragon*. There were old telephones and video games. On the wall there were a couple old army uniforms.

They were pretty low-key evenings. It was nice to be around lots of like-minded people. It also broke up the week. They were nights you didn't mind feeling the next day.

The three who visited China told us it was awesome. They went to the Great Wall. They had Peking duck. John found strong over-the-counter drugs that made him semi-unable to do things. They took a sleeper train to Xi'an, the old capital. They saw the Terracotta warriors. Donna said they were smaller than she expected.

Donna asked how my vacation was. I told her it was okay. It wasn't much of a trip, but at least now I could find my way around Busan.

"I'm a little jealous," I said.

"*It was so amazing,*" she replied.

We talked about what we'd do for Chuseok, Korea's Thanksgiving. The three who went to China were just going to chill. The girls thought they might head down to Busan to sit on the beach. So, it would be Ben, Brian, Mark from England and I. We'd catch a train sometime in the morning. We'd make a go of it. We'd meet at McDonalds or the GS. Brian wanted to pick up a camera. I didn't care where I went. Ben wanted to hit the rides at Lotte World. Mark from England couldn't shut up about the places he wanted to go.

24

I didn't know how hard it would be to get a haircut. I saw what could happen. I worried for weeks that I would come out looking like Kim Jong Il. Most of the guys went to a place called Blue Club. This would be my first haircut in months. With the heat being nearly unbearable everyday, I had reached the tipping point.

I found a few photos in the *National Geographic* I could take to show the stylist, but in the end I thought it best to just draw something. I gave it to the lady who sat me down. In the end, she cut it a little too short. I looked like a soldier.

Growing up I remember dreading having to listen to the guy who cut my hair. I couldn't stomach the small talk, and the stories he probably told everyone who came in. This time, at least, it was amusing to fumble around using sign language and a picture to make sure the stylist didn't wreck my style. Luckily I didn't have much to lose.

Walking out of the barbershop feeling relatively well put together I saw Donna. She was on her way back from the night before. She had just spent a large sum of money on a cab ride back from a party in the sticks, in a place called Gumi. It was a hell of a long way away.

She said she fell asleep in the taxi and didn't wake up until she was outside Homeplus. She tried to give the man $10 but, he said 'No, $150.' She couldn't understand him at first she was so out of it. He had to write down the amount.

The cab driver waited while she went into a bank to withdraw the cash. She said he was pretty cool about it. She must have been desperate to get home.

I told her she smelled terrible. She told me to fuck myself. I thought she was what it would look like if women ruled the earth.

We didn't talk long, but we arranged to meet to go to Costco to get supplies for a dinner I told everyone I'd make.

I said I'd make fajitas. I'd been craving Mexican food and there wasn't a restaurant in Daegu that had anything decent. She said she'd help me out. Everyone else volunteered to bring something.

"See you later then," I said.

"All right handsome, see you soon."

I met her again a few days later. We caught a taxi to Costco, just across the river from Chilgok.

I didn't mention the taxi ride from Gumi, but I couldn't wipe the smile of my face. She gave me a suspicious look.

She was close to her family. She was the oldest of three girls. She said she was a little bit of a tomboy growing up. Her dad took her to San Francisco Giants games. She told me he recently got back from a vacation somewhere in Bolivia where he shot hundreds of doves.

She and Ben were good friends. They shared a love of baseball. We were both a little concerned about him. He didn't look like he had slept in a month. Nobody really got a chance to see behind his sunglasses. I wondered what he did with his time. He was almost finished his year. He would be leaving soon.

Donna was almost done too, as it turns out. She'd be on her way to Thailand at the end of October.

She said, "I don't know what I'm going to do. I am going to Thailand when I am finished. My parents are going to meet me. I am going to spend some time scuba diving and smoking dope."

At Costco we picked up what we needed. I found cheddar cheese, fajita spice and avocados. Everything else for my Mexican meal I could grab close to home.

I also found maple syrup from Canada. I grabbed a 2L bottle. Donna said, "You and your fucking maple syrup."

Everything else went well. We split a bag of frozen spinach and cheese stuffed ravioli and a two pack of pesto.

We caught a cab back to the Gok. She had me get out first. She said she wanted to see where my apartment was so she could find it that weekend.

I taught school the rest of the week. I was on my way to Homeplus on Saturday when I ran into Ben and Mark from England. They were standing outside the Dunkin Donuts. It was raining slightly. They didn't have umbrellas, so we decided to sit down inside.

"Christ, what happened?" I asked.

"Long story," Ben said.

"I got time."

He explained that he hadn't slept in days. He said that he and Mark were downtown and they just hadn't stopped. He had no idea where they'd been.

He remembered hanging out with a group of hip-hop dancers in a subway station. He bought a tennis ball, two golf balls and a plastic Puma shopping bag from an old man sometime during the night. He said he was ready for Seoul.

Mark rolled a tennis ball around the coffee shop. Ben explained that they'd tried everything possible to lose it. He said at one point they stood on either side of an expressway and played pass while traffic rushed by.

Now they were seeing how people reacted to the ball. They rolled it around people. They rolled it through their legs. Most people would ignore them, but sometimes they cracked a smile. No one had gotten angry yet.

Mark from England seemed to be reacting like a normal human who hadn't slept all night. He was slow, but he was also funny and talkative. He was different.

The sleep deprivation worked different on Ben. He was relatively lucid. He seemed to become more himself. He spoke eloquently for someone who had been drinking nonstop for at least a day.

He said he'd had his fill of Korea. It was a good time. He'd met a few interesting people.

He said, "I work in a big school. Recently there's been a change in the people coming over. I can't explain it. I have to listen to some pretty mindless shit."

I nodded.

He continued, "This coworker went to Thailand. I heard her talking about swimming in the hotel pool, free popcorn in the hotel lobby and which programs were on HBO... What's the fucking point?"

"Don't cut your ear off," I said.

"I want to be the guy those people point to and say, 'we're not all like that.' *That* would please me," he finished.

I invited them both to dinner the next day and left them on their way.

The next day I readied dinner with Donna. She joined me to help set everything up. She was jealous of the size of my apartment. Compared to some of the other teacher's places mine was palatial. She showed me her mom's guacamole recipe. I made her pull the heads off the shrimp. She was a trooper.

A good group of people turned up. Besides Donna and I, there was Crystal, Brian, Mike from Maryland and his date, Mike and Lindsay, Ian the Australian and Mark from England. I was a little disappointed that Ben didn't come, but I understood. It just wasn't his scene.

I liked to get everyone together. There was wine, beer and a bottle of tequila to go with the fajitas. I had a white board and markers from school to keep everyone occupied. They wrote cute messages like, 'Dan is gay.'

We sat around eating, drinking and being merry. This time most everyone left early. The next day we all had to work. I told them I would try to have another dinner soon.

25

One especially hot night, Crystal had a few people over for drinks. Her apartment was on the other side of town. It was a cozy little place. We listened to music and kept the neighbors awake. At that point, Crystal was deeply in love with the Killer's song "For Reason's Unknown." She played it a few times. I think being in Korea was getting her down.

Donna and I walked home after. We were both pretty gone. As we got closer to our end of town, we decided to stop outside a GS for a nightcap.

I told her a little about my life growing up. I said I was the middle child. My brother and sister both had similarly large personalities, though other than that they couldn't be more different. They clashed often. It was up to me to make sure they didn't take things too far.

I thought maybe I was suited to a career in negotiation. I calmed down a few nasty disputes in my time. I thought about going into law like my brother. I told her my brother was doing well and that some day he would do something great. I hoped I wouldn't be his Roger Clinton.

I told her about the summer before Korea. I was finishing school and working full time. I wrote papers on Nietzsche's philosophy and labor issues in *Office Space* and *Robocop*. I'd really challenged myself. I only had two semesters before graduation. After that, I was free.

The fall semester I had another full course load, I was played on a decent hockey team, I had a girlfriend and, on top of that, I was working nearly full time.

One day in late September I finished school and stopped by my parent's house. It was one of those perfect late summer days.

My mother's truck was in the driveway. I didn't know who was driving it. I didn't know who would be home. My dad's new boat still took up too much room in the driveway.

124

I went upstairs to their sun deck. I walked through the door into the kitchen. No one answered when I said hello. I went to the fridge to get something to drink. I poured a glass of iced tea.

I noticed the windows were wide open. It smelled like someone had been cleaning. When I lived there they had been vigilant about closing windows and locking doors, whenever no one was there. I thought maybe they were around talking to one of the neighbors, but they usually wouldn't leave the house for long. I went outside on their comfortable deck and sat down.

I was flipping through a newspaper when my aunt pulled in to the driveway. She was with my grandmother. I said hello to them and told them to come up on the deck. I walked down the back stairs to say hello and my grandmother stopped me. My aunt walked right by.

My grandmother said calmly, "Dan, I've got to tell you something..."

In a moment my mind filled with scenarios that seemed unimaginable only a heartbeat before. *Someone is dead - my dad in a car accident on the way to work - my mother - not my brother or sister. Don't let it be any of them.*

Thankfully, I wasn't right. It turns out my mom had a reaction to the medicine her doctor prescribed her for depression. Later he would admit he didn't use the best judgment. The drugs made her go off.

She tried to kill herself. She took the whole bottle and called my grandmother in a daze. She immediately recognized something was wrong and raced over to make sure everything was okay. She said I didn't need to know anymore of the details.

My grandmother said she was okay. She was in the hospital. She was there for a few days.

My mother was always a very strong. She had to be. She was a business agent for a major labor union. Her job involved helping worker's with conflicts they had with management. All to often, she got it from both sides.

Despite fighting an uphill battle everyday, she'd always come back for more. Although it is obvious how thankless her job could be, she worked harder than anyone I knew. As a kid you couldn't help hearing about the garbage she had to put up with. Anytime she answered the phone she would light a cigarette. The phone rang often.

I wasn't prepared to take it on. It took days to get my head straight. I replayed things she said to me earlier that day on a phone call we had. Everything seemed normal. I never suspected a thing.

When she returned home from the hospital her and my dad asked me not to tell my brother and sister. At the time, he was working back East and she was vacationing in Mexico. They didn't have a clue what happened. I went along for a while, but it was a lot to deal with..

The rest of the year I put my head down and got through school. For months I pushed everyone away. I had to get through school to earn my ticket out of dodge.

"Pretty messed up, huh?" I finished.

"Have they found out what's wrong with her?" Donna asked.

"She thinks they have, but you can't be sure. She's seen plenty of doctors. They think it is bipolar disorder. That's the name they are giving it."

"Wow."

"Yeah."

"At least she's not transsexual."

"Thanks."

"Anytime."

"How many doves did your dad say he killed?"

I told her I worried that I still bottled things up. She said she couldn't see it. She said I looked pretty laid back. People always said that about me. Either way, I felt fortunate to come all the way around the world and meet someone like her.

26

Near the end of September everyone had a week off for Chuseok. During this time many Koreans visit their ancestral homes and perform ceremonies.

Everyone met at Wabar after work on Friday. We ironed out the details – when and where to meet. Brian said he found a hotel in Seoul. I didn't prepare anything.

We left early on Saturday. We met at the GS and walked down to Homeplus. I got coffee at McDonalds. It was good and strong. After, I went to the alcohol section with Brian to pick up some Bailey's. He grabbed a bottle of Johnny Walker Red. I was pretty confident my choice wouldn't last long, but thought it was a little early for something amber.

It was refreshing to wake up early. Outside, it was overcast and warm. It looked as if it might even rain. I didn't see many mornings the first few months I was there. Those I had seen were a result of drinking until the sun came up.

After we bought drinks and supplies we caught a cab down to Dongdaegu Station. Everyone was excited to get out of the Gok.

The KTX shot us up to Seoul. The ride was pleasant enough. We all sat back enjoying the whiskey and Irish cream in our coffee. Outside, it began to clear up as the train swept northward. The train crossed through hills and plains and made stops in a few smaller cities. It didn't take long before we crossed over the Han River into the city.

As the train approached the station I tried to remember specific landmarks, but the city was massive and overwhelming. The train slid into the station and we set out to find the hotel. The new station was packed with people.

Brian was the man with the plan. We got a cab to our hotel. It was tucked away on a side street near Insadong.

After that, we got ourselves in order, having a few more drinks to ease into the day. We'd already finished the

Irish cream and whiskey and it was time for more. Luckily in Seoul you can find it every ten steps.

We made our way to Namdaemun Market. Luckily, there were three or four camera stores still open. It seemed that most everything was closed for the holiday. Brian picked up his new Nikon, while the rest of us waited. After that, we quickly set out to put it to use.

We headed to Gyeongbok Palace. Gentle hills rise up behind it. There were a few clouds high in the deep blue sky. It was pleasant weather.

We were lucky to see the changing of the guards in the courtyard in front of the south gate. They wore bright, multi-colored traditional outfits.

There was an enormous, wooden building in the center of the complex that everyone walked toward, but we just walked around. I was very impressed by the site, but my mind wasn't right for exploring.

We left Brian, who was busy taking pictures with his new camera, to find somewhere quiet. Considering we'd all been putting back whiskey since the morning, there wasn't much enthusiasm for anything besides finding a place to relax. The three of us walked around until we found a quiet courtyard where we finished our bottle.

We sat in the shade of a large red pine. Kids came up to say hello. Then more and more people set up shop, so we moved on and found a spot where we could toss around Ben's tennis ball.

We were standing admiring some white and red carp swimming in the pond that surrounds Gyeonghoeru Pavilion when Brian found us. He was disappointed to see that the whiskey was gone.

It was the first palace I'd ever seen in my life. It was a good start to the day.

Next, we made our way on foot to Insadong, an area full of restaurants and shops that sell antiques and souvenirs.

We looked around. We took care of some administration. We posed for photos next to pieces of street art.

After dinner, at a decent Indian restaurant, we sat on the street and a boy with a bow and arrow posed for Brian. His little arrows had rubber suction cups. He shot a poster of a girl in a red bikini just over my head.

Ben took us to play games at an arcade. He played Altered Beast, an old Sega game. I watched for a few minutes, but I could only stay for so long. In Korea it is usually loud enough outside. This arcade was disorienting.

Brian and I waited for him near a punching game just outside the entrance. It was the same game that we had at the batting cage in Chilgok. Young men charged at it and swung with all their might, hoping for a high score.

When Ben finally came out Brian took us to a batting cage down the street. The whiskey had mostly worn off. I lost my grip a few times because of the humidity. The bat went flying out to where the balls filtered. I thought I better stop before I killed someone.

We decided to head to Itaewon. American soldiers stationed at nearby Yongsan Garrison contributed significantly to the culture and nightlife. The Korean media often reported soldiers beating taxi drivers, sexually assaulting women and fighting in the bars and on the streets here.

It's not all bad. There are shops you don't see everyday. You can find decent cigars. John said he bought black market Detroit Lions NFL jerseys somewhere in the labyrinth of shops. You could find just about anything if you had the time. If you were into it, you could walk up Hooker Hill to meet a girl. At the top was also Korea's best English bookstore.

We stopped in a few places.

"Feels like East St. Louis," Brian remarked.

It wasn't long before we went back to the hotel. I crashed, but the boys stayed up.

The next day we were going to go to Lotte World, an amusement park in the west end of the city. When I woke up I went to the other room and found Ben curled up in bed sheets like he'd taken a vial of something. A little before noon we made our way out of the hotel. I was amazed he had pulled himself together. We were all maintaining relatively well.

We caught the subway to Lotte World. At one point the train emerged from the darkness and I looked out at the city. As far as I could see there were white buildings jammed into the flat land around the hills.

The train was packed. It seemed the entire train exited at the Lotte World stop. It felt as if every young person in Korea was there.

The wait for rides was grim. The wait for beer was tolerable. We all carried out our limit each time we got in line.

I mostly watched Brian take photos. I was really impressed with what he could do with a camera.

"Drinking steadies the hands," he told me.

There were a few carnival games to keep us amused. I tried my luck at the high striker. The hammer grip was slick. I thought I might not be able to hit the small target. The crowd was large. I didn't want to have the marker tell me I was 'Puny' or 'Feeble.' I connected with the first swing, but I had to take a lot off. I almost missed it on the second swing. I felt a strong desire to wash my face.

On the way out, we took pictures inside the giant complex. On an ice arena at the center, a few floors below, I saw a girl practicing figure skating. She looked like Yuna Kim.

We went back to Itaewon. We drank more. We walked up Hooker Hill. We walked down Hooker Hill. We sat on a balcony overlooking the madness.

In all directions there were lonely, dead-end people. Below us a tiny blonde girl sat with her head between her legs. Police stood on the street corner looking beguiled.

The next day we headed over to the War Museum. On the way we stopped by Insadong where Ben picked up a hat that read, "All Day Drunken." It was as accurate a saying as I have seen.

I've always wanted to find something like that to describe me. I usually settle on clothing with no logos.

At the museum we checked out some outstanding photography from the war, showing all the devastation. One that stood out was a photo of a group of Canadian soldiers playing hockey on a frozen river.

After we went outside and explored some of the vehicles used in the war. There were all sorts of planes and helicopters.

I saw a giant black and yellow spider set up on a fence. I tried to take a photo with my camera. I couldn't seem to get a clear shot no matter what I tried. Then, Brian took a photo of the spider that was so vivid it made me decide to buy a better camera.

We didn't have time to explore more than a few exhibitions. Brian and I decided to come back when we both had the chance.

There wasn't much left to do in Seoul. I was beat. We caught the KTX back to Daegu. As the train got moving, I noticed Ben was finally asleep.

27

The summer was slowly coming to a close and daily life started to follow more or less the same routine. The students always kept me on my toes. Each child brought a different challenge. Some were quiet, others couldn't stay in their seats and some knew all the answers. Every day had its share of successes and failures.

I learned to simplify things, to speak slower and be more patient. I tried to have the children reason and form an opinion. Some children had a good idea of Korea's place in the world. Other kids refused to believe that Korea was smaller than Canada. It had more people. I'd give them that.

Some kids couldn't be bothered to listen to my lessons. I hoped they'd come around. Others worked hard. They were easy to be around.

There were lots of different media to keep the kid's attention. Using the large LCD screens in my classroom I could always put on a decent presentation. I drew maps and pictures on the whiteboard. If I had a little time left over I'd follow it up with something from YouTube. I would show clips like, "Dan Osman at Lover's Leap." It was a great feeling to see the children's eyes widen.

The greatest pleasure I received came when a student asked a question that went beyond, "How are you?"

I remember a tiny elementary school girl ask me, "Why did you come to Korea to teach?"

I couldn't answer her straight off. Her words caught me off guard. I was teaching kids years older than her who didn't use more than a few simple phrases, even after years of attending English academies. Few children had her ability. Fewer still cared to actually ask a question.

When the surprise wore away I didn't have an answer for her. I tried to feed her something simple, but even then I couldn't find the words. It didn't seem right to tell her that I was fascinated by Korea. That was untrue. I didn't want to tell her it was because I couldn't get a similar job in Canada. I didn't want to tell her that the strongest reason I had to come was that the job paid a decent wage comparable to other places in the world or that I thought I could use Korea as a jumping off point to see the more interesting parts of Asia. Her question was too complex for me to give her an answer she'd understand. The truth is I didn't really pick Korea.

I answered, "That's a great question."

I could sense her disappointment. I could tell she wasn't amused. She grimaced like Lisa Simpson - too bright for her own good. I felt sorry for kids like her. They are going to go through life unfulfilled with all the pat answers given by people who are expected to know better.

During another lesson on frequency adverbs with a different class, we discussed 'sometimes,' 'often,' 'always,' and 'rarely.' Through an open window you could begin to hear the air peel, like slow rolling thunder, and then a line of fighter jets passed over our school. The sound echoed off the buildings in the area. One boy said, "Always USA is fight."

I could hardly argue with him.

Lance returned from China to pick up the belongings he left with Mark from England. He had a full red beard. His old boss bought him a wide, pink and purple striped tie as a going away present. He wore it out to dinner.

He said he had a wild time in China. He had enough bizarre stories from his brief time there he could write a novel. I decided I'd head there the first opportunity that I had.

We went to Joe's for barbeque. It was Brian, Ben, Lance and I. They reminisced about the year. Lance said the highlight of his year in Korea was visiting North Korea.

He said, "I expected at some point I'd be kidnapped."

Ben said he had a lot of memories, good and bad. He learned to lower his expectations. He said, besides the friends he'd made, the thing he'd miss most was his refrigerator.

It is always tough to see a good friend go, but I was happy for Ben. He was a smart guy. He could've done anything, yet he chose to come here.

I wish I could remember better some of the conversations we had. He had an interesting take on things, but more than anything he was honest.

There was a good-sized crowd for his goodbye party on a Tuesday at Wabar a few weeks later. He was still wearing sunglasses. I looked over at him, wondering where he was.

I didn't feel much like drinking, so I waited for a chance to say goodbye.

"It was a pleasure."

"All mine, Danny Boy."

"It isn't going to be the same."

"Change is change."

He left me a copy of *Zen and Motorcycle Maintenance*. Strangely, my brother also gave me a copy a few years before.

I've never read the book all the way through, though I remember a passage where the main character sits on his motorcycle on a country road observing people stuck in traffic. They are on a freeway, but the cars are not moving. Inside, the commuter's faces are twisted with frustration.

It made me think the secret is to find my own best way. I was pretty sure he would find his.

Things quieted down noticeably, after Ben's departure. Summer was over. I remember the weather was finally pleasant. There were long stretches of weeks without rain. Living on the south coast of British Columbia all my life, I never knew such weather existed.

There was very little stress. I went to the bank. I taught. I read a few books. Days became shorter and shorter. Most days I was left alone with my thoughts.

Unfortunately, it wasn't long before Donna took her leave. Her plan was to go to Thailand and then head back to California to see friends and family and figure things out.

Before she left, Crystal got everyone to shoot a farewell video for her. I said my part and forget the next day what I said. What can you say?

On Halloween Crystal showed everyone the finished product. Near the end of the video, Ben came on and said some kind words. Wherever he went he stole the show.

Donna was in tears. Her mascara ran. She told us before her costume was, 'The Walk of Shame.' Her hair was matted and mussed. Her shirt was ripped, revealing a little hot pink bra. A condom stuck to the ass of her hiked up skirt. What a package.

She said her replacement was unreal. The first day he came to work in biker shorts. She could hear Madonna's "Material Girl" buzzing from his headphones. I saw him biking around town a few times. I was sad to see her go.

All the leaving gets you down. It is disorienting. It is hard when you find a great friend and then watch them walk out of your life, possibly forever.

I started to realize that it was important to put away some money. I didn't want to continue paying student loans after I left. I didn't have hulking payments, but they ate away a little each month.

I needed a little more structure. I decided to find a decent gym. I didn't want to come back to Canada fat and poor.

Thursdays became more important. The camaraderie with other English teachers made it an easier time. A chap from England took Ben's spot. He was a nice enough guy. He came out once or twice with Ian.

Much of my leisure time was spent playing pool with Brian. We'd talk about life. He said his family was doing well enough. His dad was a well-known theatre director who had worked all over Canada. Before that, he worked as a used car salesman in Saskatchewan. Brian grimaced when he talked about the years in his childhood when his father was known around town as "Lowball McHale."

I told him my dad worked in a youth prison for 30 years.

We talked about Canada. It's a tremendously beautiful place, but we'd both obviously had trouble finding our place there. He didn't know what he was going to do when his contract was up either. Things didn't look promising. He thought about heading to Vancouver to look for something.

Every weekend we wandered downtown. We found a few places to pass the time.

One favorite was a place called Billibow. The bar's main draw was a game that was a combination of billiards and bowling. With a pool cue you knocked your ball down a long, narrow lane toward miniature bowling pins. Your score appeared on the screen the same as regular bowling. Our games were usually quite competitive and it was free to play. You only needed to buy drinks. It didn't take much to convince us to stay.

In late November we decided to head back to Seoul to take a few more photos of Seoul Tower and to see a new exhibition at the War Museum. Brian said we'd meet his friend Ian there. We could stay at his apartment. It was a little train ride south of Seoul in a place called Pyeontaek. I didn't bother looking for things to do while we were there. I thought it was good enough just to get out of dodge.

We met his friend at Seoul Station. He seemed like a decent guy. He'd been in Korea for five years. He and Brian met a year or so earlier when they both taught in Daejeon.

We got in a cab and went back to the War Museum. The exhibition that we came to see had detailed displays of weapons and battles from the past. There were a few dioramas depicting battles from the Japanese invasion of 1592. Further along, there was an exhibit of a refugee village during the Korean War. The people in the scene were exceptionally lifelike. You could see what they were eating - cans of Spam and not much else.

After that we headed to Myeondong. It was already getting dark. We found a bar to kill some time. It was much colder in the city than our last visit. It felt like winter.

We went back to the station to catch a train for Pyeongtaek. We passed around a bottle of whiskey standing in the space between the cars.

Through a window I could see the evening's lights pass by. As we went farther down the track the lights became more sporadic. Between the light and dark very little was revealed.

Every now and then the train approached a station near a suburb. Past the flashing neon signs, of convenience stores and fast food joints, I could see a blue glow coming from distant apartment blocks along with a peppering of neon orange crucifixes.

Less and less people stood with us, the further away from Seoul the train travelled. Suddenly it was our stop.

28

Pyeongtaek lies next to the ocean on a coastal flat where wind sweeps across from the Yellow Sea. It was the worst place I've ever spent a night in my life.

Inside the train station there were quite a few migrant workers. Ian said they were employed in factories around the city. They come from poorer places in Asia. In this way it was one of the most diverse places in Korea.

We walked a minute away from the station into the Red Light District. There was an entire neighborhood full of tiny shops. All the windows were decorated with playful heart and bunny graphics. Girls sat inside, 1 or 2 in each shop. There shadows fell on the unpaved street. Pimps in shiny grey suits stood at either end.

Vancouver has its own problems. Driving in from the suburbs, you couldn't miss seeing girls working just off Hastings. I remember that William Pickton was on trial at the time for murdering women he picked up there.

In front of me, everything was arranged so it felt almost like walking through a factory.

Burger King was a short walk away. We sat and drank flat cola with our value meals. It felt like a sick twist on the American Dream.

To get to Ian's apartment, we crossed a river on our way from the station into another part of the city to the west. A new U.S. Army Base dominates this section of the city.

Ian's flat was in a quiet area. It was a little walk from the main strip. The interior was depressing. There were patches of mold on the walls. He had a scared little dog that peed on newspapers set here and there.

We drank North Korean soju that he got on a trip across the DMZ. Not long after that we went out to see the town. It was a short walk. The streets all around the main strip close to the base were being rebuilt. The ground was ripped apart and uneven. All around there were shadowy storefronts and patches of neon.

There were a few young soldiers and their ladies next to a beat-up old Hyundai, outside a GS25. It was the brightest shop in the whole area. One of the girls was Russian by the sound of it. One soldier eyed us like he was still carrying a weapon.

"Don't worry about us. We're English teachers from Canada," I thought to say.

We went to a bar on the south side of the strip. Ian said they had girls from the Philippines.

The bar was dark. There were others I'd never care to meet drinking just beyond, where there is no light. It was a dive in the meanest sense. I can't imagine a place more abysmal. It was like the Mariana Trench with smoke.

A girl took our order. Ian said we had to order one for her.

We played pool on a ragged table. She played with us. She told us she came here to make money for her family back home. She told us most of the other girls tried to do the same. Ian knew who she was. He said he came by every so often.

We went to another place, a dark hole in the wall that played old rock and roll. We played darts and drank Jagerbombs. You couldn't find Redbull or Jagermeister where Brian and I lived in Daegu. We went round after round for about an hour. The jolt of sugar, caffeine and liquor was a godsend. It slowly took over, leaving me numb.

It was the only way to get through the nightmare outside. I wished it would knock me out. I wanted the whole night to be erased. I wanted to wake up somewhere else.

We went to one more place. It was a little more inviting. There were a few troops out past curfew. It was still late, but they were mellow. Brian and I sat down while his friend talked to the owner.

"We'll get out of here early," Brian said.

"When's the first train?" I asked.

"Hellhole, isn't it?"

"I don't want to touch anything."

Most people were friendly, but it wasn't hard to see through it. On the strip that leads to the army base, bartenders smile as they pour spirits and girls do their best to sell their bodies without losing theirs.

We were emptying our glasses when a fight started at the bar. Ian screamed, "I'll rip your fucking head off!"

Brian was keeping an eye out for his friend. It could have escalated quickly, if he hadn't stepped in. Luckily, the fight was broken up before it started.

Two fresh pints arrived at our table. Brian said he'd take Ian outside to cool off. I turned to another fellow who helped break up the scuffle and offered him a beer.

I asked him what he did here. He said he was a teacher. He'd spent time in the army before that.

I told him my impression of Pyeongtaek. I wondered how such a place came to exist. He raised the corner of his mouth into a half smile.

He explained that most of the Korean girls were involved because they were addicted to expensive handbags, clothing and plastic surgery. They ran up unsurmountable bills on their credit cards. Soon their debt was far beyond what they could afford. They had very little alternative except to turn to prostitution. Some girls worked at singing rooms. Some girls worked at bars. There were endless ways.

He said the reach of the sex trade was staggering. Just about everywhere you looked it took place. You just had to know what to look for. He said some people accused both the U.S and the Korean governments of facilitating the trade in young girls to sustain the morale of the troops stationed in the country. At first Korean girls serviced the boys, but gradually the system developed. He said now mostly Filipino and Russian girls serviced the soldiers. A large number of boys came straight from tours in Iraq and Afghanistan looking for love. As long as there were troops cycling through the peninsula, there would be a healthy sex trade.

He finished saying, "The bases here aren't going anywhere."

I was beginning to lose the little focus I had left. I saw Brian outside propping Ian up against a vending machine.

Time to go.

I was extremely relieved to be walking down the dark, dirty road back to somewhere I didn't have to be on my guard. The moldy piss smell of Ian's apartment was almost welcome. Either way, it was quiet. Sleep came like a gift.

Brian and I stood between the compartments on the train back to Seoul. I was happy to move further and further from Pyeongtaek. I felt very fortunate about where I was living.

I looked for something beautiful and unique in the landscape to make me forget where I had just come from. Unfortunately, we were headed back to Seoul.

I asked Brian about his friend. He told me that Ian couldn't handle his liquor very well to begin with, but he'd just split with his girlfriend. She went back to Thailand. Brian said that Ian still sent her cash.

"What a sucker," I said.

Brian nodded.

We agreed that living in Pyeongtaek couldn't help. It was all I could do to stay for one night. I didn't know how anyone would move halfway around the world to live in such a place.

We hung around Seoul during the day. We made our way from Itaewon to Seoul Tower. We wanted to go up to take a few photos of Seoul at night. It was cold, but we walked up the hill.

We arrived at the top at sunset. From the top of the tower you could see buildings and lights and signs.

We walked back down in the frigid cold. We made our way through Namdaemun Market. We passed through alleyways filled with food stands. There were vendors barbequing skewered chicken and green onions in soy sauce. Others scooped rice cakes simmering in red pepper sauce. There were a number of shops displaying glowing vats of golden ginseng.

We caught a slow train back to Daegu. I was wide-awake. During the long ride, I almost finished reading *Cat's Cradle* by Kurt Vonnegut.

We continued our routine of BilliBowl and Pool. I could always count on him for an evening of drinking and conversation. He already knew the deal about Asia. He'd been here awhile. He saw behind the facade. He said, "You have to take it all lightly, if you don't you'll go off."

One day we found a Playstation2 room on one of our walks downtown. We both thought it was a great idea. It had large screen TV's and comfortable chairs. We settled on playing baseball after a couple rounds of boxing.

Because baseball can be tedious, we played home run contests while mixing cheap whiskey with Dr. Pepper. We set the game to Fenway Park, so we could see how many balls we could hit over the Green Monster. To make things more interesting we decided the loser of each match should take a nip.

We were alone aside from a group of college students sitting beside us playing "FIFA World Cup Soccer." Each time they scored they erupted in screams and wails.

The first time it happened we looked at each other. Unfortunately, it happened again and again until Brian stood up and told them to quiet down. They were far too ecstatic for such a confined space.

We were both a long way from being passionate about computer games. We wanted quiet. We wanted to relax in the dark room, sitting in our reclining seats watching a big screen.

Unfortunately, the game room was like 99% of the places in the downtown, you just couldn't chill.

Brian said, "I can take a lot of shit. I can handle teaching my boss's precocious children. I can handle when he throws a tantrum because he doesn't get his way. I can take businessmen calling me names that they think I don't understand. I've managed not to punch any of the belligerent assholes that come up to me and say 'hello' like it's some sort of game. It's not cool anymore. It's not cool. I've been a nice guy. You can't be a gentleman here. I've fucking had it. I'm done."

29

Everything progressed smoothly through into December. Those of us who were left continued to have dinner at Joe's on Thursday. Now those nights all seem like one.

We all had two extra days off to celebrate Christmas. I said I would have people over to my place for dinner. A few days before some of us went to Costco. There was no turkey. We settled on steak. I told everyone to bring wine.

On Christmas Eve we had a party at Crystal's. She went all out. There was homemade eggnog. There were red lights. There was Christmas music.

She told us that during the week leading up to Christmas her manager instructed her to refrain from singing Christmas tunes around the office. She was told that it took away from her teaching.

We had a game of Secret Santa. I ended up with a tea set. I put it to good use later on. Ian from Australia ended up with a soju set. He was not impressed. Just after he got to Korea, he said he would never touch the stuff. I don't know what he did with it.

Most of us there were from the GOK. Brian's friend made it down from Pyeongtaek. I was happy for him getting away from that place.

A cute Korean English teacher was also there. I talked with her. She said she would show me her side of town someday. She left the party early. The rest of us finished the night playing Jenga and tipping over wine glasses.

On the walk back to our end of town Brian, his friend and I stopped off at a tented restaurant. We ordered kimchi jigae, a spicy stew. We downed a little soju with some young Korean folks. It was near first light. It was Christmas in Korea.

I went to Brian's for breakfast around noon. We had Canadian bacon and eggs. We had Bailey's in our coffee.

Brian's friend brought a few bags of Tim Horton's coffee. The breakfast was pretty outstanding.

It didn't take long to throw together Christmas dinner. Around dusk everyone showed up. I rolled up my sleeves. Crystal helped a lot. If it weren't for her I couldn't have consumed nearly as much wine. I hoped the dinner was good.

After dinner most of us walked to the reservoir near Hamjisan and lit fireworks. I took a picture of Crystal and Mark standing in front of a neon green swastika, the buddhist symbol for eternity. The searing green symbol rested above their heads like a halo.

When we ran out of things to light, a few people went home. The rest of us proceeded to the batting cage across town.

Christmas came and went quickly. The next day we all had to work. It was strange spending the holiday season in such a different place.

Usually on Christmas I played football with friends. It was going to be the first time I hadn't played in almost a decade. It was strange to be away, but I was comfortable. I had made good friends in a short time. I had a lot of reasons to be thankful.

New Year's Eve was uneventful. I had to work. A few people went to Busan to drink and have a good time lighting more fireworks on the beach. I downloaded *Empire of the Sun* and *I, Robot*. While I tried not to think of the fun I was missing, it was refreshing entering a new year with a clear head.

At school, 'Winter Camp' started the first week of January. I came up with the idea of studying UN Heritage Sites. I decided I'd try to teach the children something that would challenge and fascinate them. I wanted them to understand the difference between cultural and natural world heritage sites.

They seemed to have such a limited worldview. I don't know if mine was as narrow when I was their age. They seemed so sheltered. I wanted them to have something to aspire to. I wanted to expand their minds.

I prepared videos and lists of vocabulary. I wrote brief articles covering each site. There was only time for one site per lesson so it was easy to find places worth exploring. I was happy to hear the kids use some of the expressions that I taught them. It was amusing to listen to the children pronouncing places like Machu Pichu, Taj Mahal and Mt. Everest.

The extra money that I received for winter camp paid for a new Nikon DSLR. It became a constant companion. It was a game changer. It gave me something positive to look forward to. Perhaps the most important thing it did was force me to see the world with a different eye.

30

I talked on the phone with Emily, the Korean English teacher I met on Christmas Eve. We decided to go see a movie. We met downtown outside the newly built Lotte Young Plaza We sat and enjoyed a hot chocolate while we waited for our movie to begin.

She told me she had never met her mother. She said she was living with her grandparents now, but she felt her life was very empty. It was heavy stuff for a first date.

After the movie we walked through the downtown. Snow began to fall as we crossed over a bridge leading to Kyungbok University. She said she lived close by. I thanked for showing my some of the town. We made plans to meet again.

We decided to go on a day trip to Gyeongju, the former capital of the Shilla Kingdom. We would visit Bulgoksa Temple and Seokguram Grotto. The temple was one of the most famous in Korea and the Grotto was supposed to be a wonder.

It was a beautiful clear and crisp winter morning. We caught a bus from Dongdaegu Station. I couldn't help smiling. Your outlook changes when you spend time with a pretty girl.

For once, I didn't have to worry about getting around. She knew the local specialties and she made sure we found a few to try. She had me try Hwangnam bread, a pastry stuffed with a sweet red bean paste.

After, we walked through a market and then posed for a few photos in front of some giant golden burial mounds. Then, we caught the bus to the temple, a short distance out of town.

We took a country road down the middle of a valley. Tall mountains rose on either side. Before long we were there.

From the bus stop you walk up a gentle slope to the temple. It was tucked away at the foot of a mountain. There were lots of vendors selling snacks and souvenirs.

The temple was built around 1,500 years ago. The buildings, originally dating from around the 8th century, were completely burned during Japan's invasion in 1592.

The pond at the entrance was completely frozen. There were no flowers. The dull winter light didn't bring out the color of the buildings. Fortunately there weren't many people.

The temple was rebuilt on the original rock and cement foundation. It was mostly yellow with maroon columns. Under the curved eaves the design was meticulously crafted with colorful carvings and patterns.

We peered into all the buildings and spent time examining the paintings of old saints and teachers. There was a little area before the main building where people stacked small rocks on top of one another. Tucked in the rocks there were coins and tiny, clay Buddha statues.

We walked to a spot behind the old rock wall that looks out into the monk's quarters. I pulled her toward me. She gave me a quick, disapproving look, but she didn't resist.

"Everyone told me to stay away from you," she said.

We held hands in the shadows of two bare, aged maple trees. We watched the scene in secret. Monks in thick, grey robes went about their business. Families walked around taking in the temple. Older folks paced leisurely while children ran around. Others posed for photographs, as you do. Then she walked out ahead of me and I followed her back out into the light.

We passed through the main building. A Buddha statue covered in gold leaf sat, peering out from the center. People knelt at its foot praying. Incense burned strong and fragrant.

Outside, looking down from the veranda, there were two unique pagodas that had survived everything. Both pagodas were national treasures. One was named Seokgatap and the other Dabotap.

Emily told me about the significance of each pagoda. She said they were both built in the 8th century. The 27-foot-high Seokgatap, or Sakyamuni Pagoda, was a traditional Korean-style stone pagoda with simple lines and minimal decoration. During its reconstruction a number of treasures were discovered inside: a sutra, a sari box, silver sutra plates, and a woodblock copy of the Dharani Sutra printed sometime after 704 AD. Dabotap, or Many Treasure Pagoda, was 34 feet tall. It was dedicated to the Many Treasures Buddha, who made a prophecy about a miraculous funerary tower in the Lotus Sutra. Its image was reproduced on the 10 won coin. In contrast to Seokgatap, it was highly ornate. Its carved stones were held together without mortar and some were carved like stalks of bamboo. It is believed the chamber within probably once contained an image of the Buddha.

The complexity of the Dabotap was balanced by the simplicity of the Seokgatap. They were said to be manifestations of the Buddha's simultaneous contemplation of and detachment from the world.

At first, they caught your attention because of their sheer size, but they didn't inspire awe or wonder. However, after I understood the history of the objects it was stunning to realize how many generations had passed since their creation and how skilled the craftsmanship was so long ago. They will likely be here long after I am gone. They are a testament to the rich history and culture of Korea. They stood in stark contrast to what I had become so used to seeing outside the temple complex.

The shadows in this area of the courtyard were starting to grow long. People gathered here and there taking photos in the courtyard. We took a few more photos by a large drum and walked outside the main gate.

We found a quiet spot by a stream to have a picnic. Brown leaves crunched under our feet. The sky was still mostly blue. It was nice to be near her and listen to her talk.

Afterward, we walked back down to the bus stop to catch a ride to the grotto. It wound its way up a mountain. Below, through the thick forest of pines, you could see some of the valley. We got off the bus and made our way up down the well-worn trail. It was lined with pink, green, blue and red lanterns.

At the end there were a few buildings and up above was another building where we had to go.

The Seokguram Grotto was part of the Bulguksa temple complex. It overlooks the East Sea. It was built by Gim Daeseong and originally called Seokbulsa, or Stone Buddha Temple.

It holds a magnificent, giant Buddha statue. Emily told me that the original engineering involved to house the Buddha had not been improved upon.

She said construction at the top of Mt. Toham began in 742. The Silla court completed the grotto in 774, shortly after Gim's death. An old legend states that Gim was reincarnated for his filial acts in a previous life. The legend relates that the Bulguksa Temple was dedicated to Gim's parents in his present life while the Seokguram Grotto was dedicated to Gim's parents from a previous life.

The centerpiece of the granite sanctuary was a Buddha statue seated in the main chamber. It was 3.5 meters in height and sat on a 1.34-meter tall lotus pedestal. It was thought to represent the Sakyamuni Buddha, the historic Buddha at the moment of enlightenment. Unlike other Buddhas that have a halo attached to the back of the head, the Buddha at Seokguram creates the illusion of a halo by placing a carved granite circle with lotus petals on the back wall of the structure.

The serene, magnificent Buddha was surrounded by fifteen panels containing different statues. There were three bodhisattvas, ten disciples, and two Hindu gods along the wall of the rotunda. The ten statues of bodhisattvas, saints, and the faithful were located in niches, five on each side. Their features suggested a Greek influence. The two bodhisattvas were Manjusri and Samantabhadra. The two Hindu gods were Brahma and Indra. On the back wall of the rotunda stood a two meter tall Avalokitesvara, the Bodhisattva of Compassion. This figure was the only bas-relief facing forward. It wore a crown, was dressed in robes and jewelry and held a vase containing a lotus blossom.

Two statues from the niches and a marble pagoda that was believed to have stood in front of the Avalokitesvara were missing from the grotto and many people believed the Japanese looted them.

It was hard to imagine something so beautiful existing here. I wondered how it had been spared. The country had been invaded and ransacked so many times and still this place remained mostly intact.

It was the kind of place you wouldn't mind staying if there weren't an endless stream of pilgrims and tourists. If there weren't all the people, I think I'd end up trying to mirror the statue. The stillness of it was something to aspire to.

By this time, the sky was filled with clouds. There was a chill in the wind that started to pick up as we posed for photos. We walked back down the trail hoping we wouldn't have to wait to long for a bus. Luckily, we caught one that was just about to pull out.

We got off at the wrong bus stop and ended up walking through the park that leads to Cheomseongdae. It was impossible to miss. Bright lights on the ground beamed upward, illuminating the 9-meter tall circular structure. No one knows for sure what its purpose was. It might have been built for the study of astrology. In Gyeongju there *were* far more stars than I was used to seeing. In the cold darkness, they sparkled.

When we got back to Daegu, we caught a taxi to Kyungbok University. Emily said she wanted to take me to her favorite restaurant.

From the north gate we walked a little way down a narrow alley lined with restaurants. Finally, she pulled at my sleeve to signal we'd arrived.

The place was tiny, but it was bustling. It was popular with students. It served jjimdak, or braised chicken with vegetables and clear noodles in a spicy soy sauce. It was a welcome meal, especially after all the walking in the cold.

After dinner, I walked her back through the school. The university was about the only place with a significant number of trees in the entire downtown. Again, it started to snow.

As it turns out, I didn't have a chance to screw anything up. She told me she was going away to Australia on a work/holiday visa at the start of February. She said she desperately needed to get out of Korea.

We stood under a leafless cherry tree. For a brief moment it was quiet. Then a group of Chinese students rolled past us, drunk and happy. It was getting late and I knew that she had to leave. I walked with her a little further until she told me to stop. I thanked her for her time. She said that she would go the rest of the way alone. Suddenly everything felt much colder.

31

I had to make a detour to avoid the owner of a Japanese Restaurant. He was getting a little too friendly. He wanted to go out and have a night drinking soju together. I didn't know how to say no. I could never go back to the restaurant again. I could no longer even walk in that direction.

I was on my way to meet Brian for our weekly pool session. Outside the GS by his school, I saw him talking to a dude wearing a jean jacket, jeans and cowboy boots. He was tall. His shoulders were broad. He was blonde. It looked like he should've been on a ranch, riding a horse or mending a fence. His name was Earl.

His girlfriend came out from the store with two cans of beer. She was a nice looking gal named Sue. She was tall and blonde, too. They worked at a university somewhere in Chilgok, in Area 1 or Area 2.

As it turns out they'd been around for a little while, I'd just never run into them. Brian said he'd met them before, but only briefly.

We grabbed a few more beers and caught an elevator up to our place with the pool table. I knew immediately that they were good people.

After pool we went to eat Haejungook. Earl and Brian started talking politics. It was interesting for a little while. The difference in political ideology between folks from Canada and Texas was pretty staggering. Earl was probably the most liberal fellow for hundreds of miles where he came from. However, Canadians, especially the type you find teaching in Korea, see things another way entirely.

I listened to Earl and Brian argue back and forth. The Texan defended his man in the White House. Earl reasoned that the U.S. had to protect itself post 9/11. It had to have a go at its enemies and also protect its strategic interests. According to him, going into Afghanistan and Iraq was a good decision.

However, he also acknowledged the human cost. He had friends who had lost their lives and others friends that came home suffering with PTSD.

I said I remembered staying awake all night watching the election Bush stole from Gore. I was unable to believe that such a man could be elected President. In a sad way it gave me hope. If someone with his past could become the leader of the free world anyone had a chance. I knew at the time it would be four dark years, but who could have predicted the turn America would take during his time in office.

There were a few things we could all agree on. We all knew that one day we'd have to pay for his orgy of destruction. Also, we must have been crazy to come to Korea.

He chuckled, "I didn't expect this. In a way, it's the freest country in the world - it's virtually lawless. If you watch an intersection for two light changes you see at least as many cars run the red. Delivery drivers on scooters jet down the sidewalk, brushing past you – you need to have eyes in the back of your head. Every night I see businessmen stumble down the street - out cold on their feet."

He paused. He gestured to the waitress to bring another bottle of soju. "I don't know. I mean, I can stand in the center of the Gok and throw a half full can of beer and hit ten different coffee shops, but not one of them can make a decent cup. I don't think I could ever come back here - not a chance."

Earl fit right in. He drank to the point of recklessness, yet I never saw him incoherent. He was mad. He had the heartiest laugh. He was the kind of person you wanted beside you going to war.

He mentioned that he and Sue were going to head off soon on a month long tour of Thailand, Laos and Vietnam. They each had six weeks off. They certainly had it over us. Brian's school gave him ten non-consecutive days off. I only had five more.

We made plans to get together when they made it back. After that we got up, paid for our dinner and posed for photos outside in the blistering cold.

The next goodbye was Brian. Obviously, I was sad to see him go. He handed me down a coffee machine, as mine had stopped working. He also gave me a chair and a wonderful reading lamp. It made my apartment far more comfy. He also left a pile of books; He gave me a stellar copy of *War and Peace*. I always wanted a quality translation of the epic. I read it a few times years before when I didn't care a thing about who did the translating.

We went downtown to celebrate Brian's birthday before he left. There was a new guy there named Scott. He was a charismatic guy from Ontario. Before going to university he played a little minor league baseball. The Texans came down. I was surprised they were still around. All in all, it was a pretty good crowd.

The Crow Bar, the place we all ended up at, never had any decent alcohol left halfway through the evening, but you could pick your own music from a list of downloaded songs, so there was always something new and different to listen to. We took pictures, played pool and drank. I remember taking a shot assuming it was tequila only to find it was 151.

It was a fun enough night, but I didn't really feel like being there. It was like the lights were on. I could see everything clearly through the fog of smoke – every bit of dirt and waste. The only way to take it was with a shot of something stiff.

The morning Brian left, I walked with him to the post office. He had to send a few boxes that he couldn't carry with him.

It was a cold January morning. There was a Siberian wind. It was clear and dry. It hadn't rained in weeks. Everyone walked fast. We shook hands and I wished him well. After that, I went to school and he went to Seoul to catch a flight back to Canada.

He said he was going to set up in Vancouver. His brother was going to meet him and they were going to stay there a little while.

I told him I'd be there in July. I thought it wouldn't be long. For a while after he left I felt a sort of malaise, but I figured it wasn't worth getting too upset. It's the nature of the job. It's inevitable that friends you make in Korea will leave. I was glad to see him get out.

One Saturday after he left I went down into Daegu with Ian and some of the newer folk. I was sitting at the bar when there was a scuffle in the corner. I saw a big fellow drop.

It turns out he pushed a girl we all knew and Ian sorted him out. I didn't know exactly what happened, but he was in a bad way. His face was bloody and he looked dazed. He wanted to stick around he was so out of it. In the end, I convinced his friend it was a good idea to look for another place. I am pretty sure he learned a lesson about putting his hand on a woman.

Ian was a tough, young fellow. He'd been with the British Army briefly. Sometimes I thought he might be a little quick to judge. This time everyone there felt he'd got it right.

Ian made friends with some of the younger teachers. He hung out with Greg, Scott, and the chap from England who replaced Ben.

We had decent conversations at Thursday night dinners. It's good to have as wide a range of opinions as possible. They were all pretty decent folk. They liked to have a good time.

Sometime later the boys had a late night on the town. They ended up in a bar near the university.

Shortly after arriving Ian and Greg were surrounded by a group of locals. Everyone spilled outside. Ian went toe-to-toe with a big boy and dropped him. He took down a few more before the commotion drew a bigger crowd. Luckily, they were able to escape. Unfortunately, the fellow from England was passed out in the bar and he took the brunt of it. His face was rearranged by a mob looking for revenge.

I learned of this the following day on Facebook. I went down and met Ian at Wabar. He told me that he was completely sober at the time. He said the big one he'd KO'd was in the hospital in a coma.

He told me that while he was in the bar one fellow said he was with the 'Busan Mafia.' He threatened to stab him. He said he was surrounded, so suddenly he had no time to think. It turns out they picked the wrong person to mess with.

The authorities sorted out everything pretty quickly and it looked like Ian was going to be on the hook for being the one to finish the fight.

The self-defense laws in Korea were pretty arcane. If you were attacked and the attacker was injured than you were still liable. The medical costs would be split.

My advice to Ian was to leave. I thought he should do a midnight run. I said he should get a train to Busan and catch the next ferry to Japan. However, he didn't want to leave. He wanted to finish his contract. There was a lot of financial incentive to stay on and finish the year. Also, I think he felt bad about what happened to his friend and he wanted to make sure everything would be okay with him. You could see the anguish in his eyes.

32

Around this time, we all had a few days off for Chinese New Year. Ian learned the Korean fellow was out of the hospital. He said he wasn't completely in the clear, but it was a giant relief. He wasn't going to jail, but his situation at work and the amount he would have to pay in blood money was still unclear. We'd planned a little trip for a few weeks and I thought it would do him some good to get out of town. We joined Crystal and Mark, who were now together, for a trip to Chungju.

We didn't plan very well. We had to stand on the train for the first leg of the four-hour journey. The train was actually packed. It was uncomfortable. Luckily, when we changed trains a few seats opened.

Outside, it was dryer and colder than where we lived in the south. Rivers were completely frozen. Higher up in the hills there was snow from days before. The sky was bright grey. It felt like it might snow.

On the train ride I saw farms, towns, military bases and prisons. There weren't any awe inspiring natural features – no great mountains or wide rivers. Everything was thoroughly tame. Nevertheless, it was nice to see a different part of the country.

Chungju is the home of Korea's largest lake. When we arrived we caught a cab across town to a quiet park next to it. We saw Korea's tallest pagoda. We posed for photos. We bought beer. We looked at the lake. Throughout the park there were giant pieces of art. We posed for photos next to them. We stopped by the World Liquor Museum, but it was closed. We quickly saw just about all there is to see.

We decided to go to Saunbo, a famous hot springs town. It was a short taxi away. There were a greater variety of stares here than any of us had experienced. Worse, the people of Saunbo seemed unaware the town was famous for anything. Judging by the baffled expression we were met with by every single person we asked for directions, the four of us might have been the town's first foreign tourists.

It took us a little time to find the Park Hotel, the only place in town with an outdoor bath. The hotel sat up on a freakishly steep hill a short walk from the center of town. It was nearly impossible to see. The interior of the hotel rivaled the place from *The Shining*. It wasn't awful, but it was dying for some attention. We had a nice long bath. I'd give the place 3 stars.

After we went to dinner at a rabbit restaurant. It was said to be the local specialty. Ian drew a picture of what we wanted - a cute little bunny. I looked forward to trying it. Unfortunately, It might've been the worst meal we'd all had in Korea. It was dry and it had far too many little bones. Still, we had a good time.

We caught another taxi back to our hotel in Chungju. Other than the outline of the brightly lit city from the taxi and Mark and Crystal's heart shaped bed, there was nothing to see. It was cold. The wind whistled.

The next morning we decided to go back to Saunbo to a nearby ski hill. It was quiet in town and everyone walked quickly. While we waited at the bus stop I took a few pictures of a giant rust-colored icicle.

We booked a hotel there for the night. The owner of the hotel was extremely gracious. He drove us in a shiny black Mercedes to the shop that rents out gear. We got outfitted and then were driven down a little hill to the ski resort. I'd never driven down a hill to go skiing.

The place was called the Blue Valley Ski Resort. It wasn't terrible. There were a few modest runs.

The others were just beginners. I left them and got in line to ride the lift to the top. I hadn't skied in years. The beginning of each run was steep enough, but it took less than a minute and I was sitting in the chair lift again. Luckily, there weren't many people waiting in line.

I talked with a few people on the chair. One man told me he lived in Vancouver for a few years. He missed the big mountains.

I did about fifteen runs in the first hour. It was nice to feel the breeze whip my cheeks a little, but I wanted something more. For the first time, I felt a strong desire to go leave.

On my last run I stopped at the top to take in the place. I could see into Saunbo. There wasn't much. In all directions there were brown and grey hills with a touch of white frosting. It was almost quiet. It wasn't exhilarating, but it would have to do.

After I'd gone down all three runs a number of times I went to see how the others were doing. It was some show.

I took them up a little hill and watched them go down. I tried to explain to move from side to side, to cut off some of the incline. Crystal and Mark cautiously made their way down, but they fell over and over again. Ian was a little braver. He went straight down, narrowly missing a number of people before bailing.

That night, at the restaurant in the hotel, we had a delicious barbeque dinner. We drank a few bottles of Baeksaeju, a sweet ginseng wine my boss got me hooked on. It wasn't to everyone's taste, but for Ian and I at least, it beat soju. Either way, they were great people to share a meal with.

Crystal and Mark had a vocabulary that was a stretch to understand. It was funny to hear their different words and figures of speech.

They referred to a costume as 'fancy dress'; swimsuits were 'swim costumes'; and a roll of toilet paper was 'a bog roll.' I hope Crystal doesn't take the piss out of me when she reads this. I don't know what it would involve.

The next day Ian and I caught a train back to the Gok. He was still agitated, and for good reason. There wasn't much I could say. He talked a little about his home. I think he'd already set his mind on leaving. He was anxious. He looked tired. Things can be stressful enough without the law leaning on you.

When we left it was sunny outside. Mark and Crystal were going to catch a bus to see a temple. She wondered about taking a pleasure cruise down the other side of the lake.

A few days later, I learned that Ian was gone. I was happy for him. If the fellow he put in a coma had somehow died, it would have been unimaginable - no one I knew wanted to stay on for a lifetime here.

33

It was still cold when the Texans returned to the Gok from their vacation. They'd been all over. Earl said he'd had a grand tour. Sue went back to Texas and then met him in Thailand.

He told me about a tube ride he took down a river in a small town in Laos. Along the way he drank a couple magic mushroom milkshakes. He said he started tripping hard while he floated down through a tranquil forest. Then, he got lost. He said he spent, what felt like, hours walking through the jungle carrying his tube, convinced he would step on a land mine. Finally, he ended up wandering into a village and was lead back to the river by a group of children.

Sue had a curious vacation. She found something that she was concerned might be skin cancer on her neck. She went back home to America to get it tested. The result was negative. It must have been quite a relief. She said she managed to spend a little time in Thailand with Earl. I was glad they were back.

We were having a few pops one Friday at Wabar when the guy who replaced Brian was dropped off by his Korean co-teacher. She knew we'd be there and pawned him off like we would take care of him because he came from America. Pretty quickly, from the odd comments he made about Koreans and Korea in general, it was clear he wasn't cool.

We all had a laugh about how people parked their cars on sidewalks. However, he gave the waitresses a hard time. He snapped his fingers for service. We had to tell him to ease up. He had no tact. He was an embarrassment.

His behavior put everyone on edge. Before long, he was rambling angrily and banging his fist on the table as if he was going to start something. Then, he said something totally incoherent, got up, and stumbled out the door. I didn't know how drunk he was. I didn't care. I was glad I could go back to enjoying my beer.

Afterward we noticed he didn't pay his tab. Earl, who had taken part in the destruction of a couple bottles of cheap tequila, wanted to teach him a lesson. I couldn't talk him out of it.

We tracked him down easily. He lived in Brian's old apartment. We knocked on his door a few times, but he didn't answer. Then, the landlady yelled at us from upstairs, so we decided to call it a night.

The tequila had done a number on Earl. The night was icy and he wore only a blue dress shirt, jeans and boots, like some sort of mutant cowboy. He had a little difficulty getting into his taxi. He wasn't completely sure which way to go. He fumbled with the pack of Marlboros he'd stored away in his shirt pocket. I pointed in the direction of his place and the taxi drove off and I stood there for a second lost in wonder.

We never saw Brian's replacement again, though, the next day, I did receive a call from the Korean co-teacher who dropped him off.

"What happened with my new co-worker on Friday night?" she asked.

I said I didn't know.

She said he was chased out of a few different places. He ended up sleeping outside his apartment because he'd lost his keys, prompting the landlady to call his boss.

I really didn't want to hear about the guy. The way I saw it, I'd replaced a quality friend with a racist West Virginian who was better served in his previous occupation, washing cars in the army. It was like the Neely trade.

About that time another couple arrived in the Gok. They were South African. They were vegetarian. Her name was Serena and his name was Bill. I heard they were thoroughly decent, outgoing people. I hoped that was true.

The first time I saw them was a Thursday at Joe's. I greeted them saying, "Not another fucking couple."

They could have taken it any way, but it turned out all right. The statement was pretty honest. There were already the English and the Texans. Now there were the SA's. It was a peculiar dynamic, but each person added something. You couldn't find a table for miles with as much diversity.

The SA's were unique. Bill was tall and slim with a big brown Lanny McDonald moustache. It looked like he stepped out of the 1970s. He was the nicest fellow. You couldn't hope to know everything that went on in his mind. He really wanted to visit Barstow. He'd catch you off guard with questions like, "What's your favorite kind of tree?"

Serena had a wicked sense of humor and she definitely was not easily offended. I'd hit the right note the first time I met them. They gave it right back. I told them if they needed anything I'd try to help.

A little while later Donna returned to Daegu. She couldn't make up her mind about what to do and she ran out of money somewhere between Thailand and Las Vegas. She returned the day after I had a quiet dinner to welcome the SA's.

That night at Wabar was one of the highlights of the winter. I was very excited, but the happiest person was Crystal. When Donna came through the door, she was in tears. She was speechless. The "Bitches on Bikes" were back in effect. The only problem was that Donna now worked in a different suburb all the way across town.

I let it slip that Brian was also coming back. He had a rough time in Vancouver and decided he'd seen enough. The rain and low grey clouds can be especially depressing. To top it all off, the only work he could find had him pouring coffee.

Donna laughed, "He's so smug. I can't wait to tease him about being a barista."

Donna told us that Ben was also considering a return. I was surprised. I hadn't heard anything from him. She told us they met in Thailand. He was having a great time there. They partied for a few days. She might be the only girl that could keep up with him.

It was a fine conclusion to the winter, all in all. The English fellow was taken care of by his school. Ian was safe in Australia. The couples were all in for Thursday nights and a few good friends were going to be around. I didn't have much time left, but it was going to be interesting.

I think I was pretty well adjusted, but I knew I could do better. I was going to the gym consistently to work off some of the anxiety that builds up when you live in a place where you can hardly communicate.

At a certain point I convinced myself the language was beyond me. I really hadn't given it much effort. Hangul, the Korean written script, was designed for easy comprehension. It is said: 'A wise man can acquaint himself with it before the morning is over; a stupid man can learn it in the space of ten days.' What was I? I guess I just couldn't be bothered. At the very least the experience taught me how it felt to be illiterate.

In life you must continue to find things to look forward to. I planned to go to China for a week. I'd always wanted to see Shanghai. I'd spend a few days there and then decide where else to go.

I still wandered around downtown Daegu looking for interesting places. I made my way to Seomun Market. It's a short walk from the center of the city. It was a large space packed with all sorts of goods.

Many people considered it the heart of the city. I think there is a lot of truth to that. At any point standing in the market you feel as if you are in the center of something.

There was said to be 4000 shops in the tiny space. You could easily get lost in the small building the market was spread around.

Outside, a few men sat and played Mahjong. Women sat and peeled garlic. Others were busy helping customers with some odd or end. I walked along fascinated by the complex organization of the area, however, I couldn't stop to gaze at any thing very long because inevitably a delivery driver on a scooter would ride up my ass.

At the more receptive stalls I would test the ladies to see if they'd give me a little something extra. Most times the effort would pay off and I could get a few extra grams of pistachios or a handful of dried fruit.

Near the end of the market you reach the meat section. It was wild. Brian told me about a friend of his who saved his student's most interesting observations. One particular line came to me when I surveyed the scene. It was a written by an elementary school boy in Mokpo, a city on the south coast. The student wrote, 'Smells have smells.'

Here, you can purchase the freshest poultry imaginable. I saw live chickens. I saw chickens being stripped to their skin. I saw chickens cut in a myriad of forms. I watched a woman break one down from wing to beak. Next to her was a stack of limp, dead birds waiting for the chopping block. Others, still alive, stepped about like caged chickens do.

Besides chickens, there was a wide range of animals on display. There were cats, dogs, and rabbits wedged into cages that were full to bursting. Pressed against the wire cages, their eyes looked dim.

Seeing animals stuffed in cages can affect people with a more sensitive disposition. In the west we are not used to seeing our food look back at us. Some people I knew who visited the market could never return. The one thing that got to me was seeing the split skull of a medium sized dog sitting on ice.

I talked to students about dog soup. As a whole, they said it was a terrible thing. They asked me if I would ever try it. I told them I made it at home. They didn't believe me.

Earl said he went for dog soup with his college students every few weeks. I remember the grin he had when he told us he'd tried some. He said it warms you up and gives you a shot of energy. He said this happened because the dogs were beaten before being slaughtered so that adrenaline runs through the meat. I hoped he was somehow wrong.

As I was leaving I saw an old man sitting on a stack of palettes. People rushed all around him. Our eyes met through the crowd of people. He had bright, innocent eyes. I wanted to ask him what he'd seen. I gave him a smile and a little wave. I think he wanted to say something, but he thought better of it. He gave a wave back. There wasn't a need for anything more. Looking back, I think we both understood.

Like anywhere there is a massive contrast between young and old. However, in Korea it felt more pronounced. Children all wore the same name brand clothes, they were shuttled from school to school and they were never more than an arm's length from a mobile phone. They complained about the hardships they had to endure like all children do. Clearly, it was a regimented life. However, there was no comparing their upbringing with that of their grandparents and those in the preceding generations.

Not long ago foreigners forced their way into the Hermit Kingdom. We have, no doubt, brought a great deal of change both positive and negative. I hoped I was doing a little part to facilitate good will.

While surfing the Internet one day I came across a story about an English teacher in Seoul struggling for his life after being caught in a fire in his apartment. It was thought he and his girlfriend were sleeping when it happened. Either way, they had almost no chance. Metal bars on the windows prevented them from escaping the fire raging outside their door. He survived though he was gruesomely burned. She might have gotten off easy, dying straight away.

Every day for a week or so I found myself searching for updates on the young man's condition. I scrolled through photos that his friends posted online. There were photos of him on his travels; there were shots taken with him in the classroom; there were photos of him with children piled on his shoulders. His life was not insignificant.

After a raucous school dinner to celebrate getting through the winter I ended up crashing at a Korean friend's.

While we were in a singing room he let it slip that he had some weed.

We went back to his place. He got out a little bag and then passed out while rolling. I finished it for him and smoked it on his balcony overlooking the city. I took another little bit for later, for a time I could better meditate on things.

When I got the chance, I shut all the windows in my apartment and turned out all the lights save for the lamp Brian gave me. I rolled a perfect joint. I thought about all the perfect joints I'd been a part of.

I thought about going somewhere, but then thought better of it. I took the opportunity to write down my thoughts, so I could remember later on.

34

On a sunny day at the start of spring I finished a workout at the gym. After, I had a refreshing sauna and steam. It was still cool outside, but it was fresh and there was a hint of warmth.

I went to a new coffee shop to get a glass of freshly squeezed orange juice. The people there were always pleasant and welcoming.

I sat down outside to enjoy my drink. I didn't have to rush to work, so I wanted to soak up as much sun as possible.

Just as I got comfortable there was an explosion. A thundering pop like no other echoed though the buildings. I turned around to see what happened and immediately I felt I had to get down. The next thing I was aware of was looking at the street with my face pressed to the ground. A few more pieces of what just happened bounced down the road.

As it turns out, a gnarly piece of shrapnel struck the wall at eye level behind where I was sitting. It left a dent in the wood exterior. I remember looking at it through the shiny metal legs of the patio furniture, as I stretched out on the ground. People came out of the shops and looked around. I picked myself up. The cafe manager tried to ask me if I was okay.

The shrapnel may have hit me in the head if I hadn't moved. I don't know for sure. It all happened so fast. I picked up the piece of metal that sat on the ground next to the cafe. A few men, a hundred meters or so down the street, were pointing up a pole toward a power transformer that was smoking. I could understand how the twisted piece of metal traveled so far. It had the weight of a football.

I walked into the school reeling. I had to talk to someone. As it turns out, the blast woke my manager who was sleeping in his office a block away. I told him what happened. He asked me if I was okay. I said, I was and I wasn't.

I was in shock. I knew what I was going through because I studied a fair amount about it during training to be a lifeguard. I didn't want to admit it, but it was obvious. My hands were shaking as I prepared for my first lesson.

I wrote the story down while I waited for class to begin. I couldn't wait to get out of class to talk with the others. I tried to put it out of my mind for the rest of the day, but it would slip back and I'd get lost thinking about what happened.

After class, I met a few friends at Wabar. I told them what happened. Bill, who has a way of putting things, said, "I don't know what I'd do if my soul stayed here."

I thought maybe I was making a bigger deal of it than I should, but there was no denying the event shook me. It is hard to look squarely at death. I don't know that I truly considered it until then. There is no reasoning your way out of it.

I tried to make my peace - I had a drink. Unfortunately, for a little while after, every time I had a few drinks I couldn't stop.

I wasn't immune to blackouts. I had drunk myself silly a few times since I arrived and too many times to count back in Canada, but after this the magnitude was amplified. I was hardly an outlier. Most of my friends had a few run-ins with the bottle during their time in Korea. The strangest part was feeling like I physically needed it. I held back once that feeling started to take hold. It scared the hell out of me.

It was hard to avoid alcohol in Korea. All the small things, the tiny inconveniences and misunderstandings stacked one on the next started to exhaust my nerves. The easiest way to cope was to knock back a few. It removed some of the weight, but it was also an illusion. I am sure there were more than a few people that came over and lost themselves.

A few days after the shrapnel incident Donna and I met to see a ball game. Unfortunately, when we got to the stadium we found it was sold out. It was disappointing to be so close.

We tried to find someone to buy tickets from, but there were no scalpers.

There were a few tall buildings surrounding the stadium that might offer a view.

I said, "We could try to see the game from a rooftop?"

"Great idea," she answered

"Of course it is."

We set off to find a view. I didn't think there was much chance we'd find anything. However, inexplicably, I saw an open door leading right into the stadium.

I don't know why someone left it open, but in an instant we were inside.

When committing a spontaneous crime it is best to move fast and act calm. We seamlessly merged into the crowd. Donna told me she hated me for making her break the law.

Inside the stadium it was madness. I knew we would be fine. People were standing everywhere. There were so many people, who would notice us?

We stood next to a ramen vendor for the first few innings. After a while a few seats opened up and we sat down and enjoyed being alone in the crowd.

We talked of things we usually would. We talked about everyone who wasn't there. She went on and on about how wonderful it was to watch a game in San Francisco. I told her about the little people after the game I watched in Seattle. We laughed at how surreal the atmosphere of a Korean ball game was. Between one of the early innings there was a beer chugging contest involving three tiny young women displayed on the giant screen. A petite little lady took down a beer in almost three seconds. Later there was a close play and the manager of the visiting team came out to argue the call. He went on and on and then walked to the batter's box and pulled the next hitter from the field. The coaches at first and third joined the rest of the team in the dugout. The game stopped for, what seemed like, an eternity. It was another made-in-Korea stalemate. We wondered if the game would be completed.

Donna said she had a great time with friends and family back in America. She went camping. She spent time at the lake. She smoked good, strong marijuana. It was a different kind of freedom.

"You do look rested," I said.

"Shut up."

She said she made a half-hearted attempt to find work in California, but nothing panned out. The only jobs were in the service industry or positions that required more schooling - another certificate or six-week course. She couldn't imagine starting at the bottom of any industry she didn't care about.

She said coming back to Korea was relatively easy. She craved the adventure. She said when she was teaching she felt somewhat engaged. She had a little control. It was the closest thing to job satisfaction she'd ever experienced. For her, there was still a little novelty being the foreign teacher that all the kids stared at in awe. She couldn't complain about the pay. She could just show up and work.

She said America's economy was grinding to a halt. The whole nation was in a sort of economic limbo. A number of her friends were hit hard by the subprime mortgage fiasco that was just beginning to unfold. A great many feared for their futures.

I wondered about Canada. I heard it hadn't been hit too hard. Still, I didn't see myself going back there other than for a brief visit. I hadn't really thought of what I might do when I returned.

I'd probably go fishing. I wanted to stand in a river. I wanted to watch puffy white clouds sweep down the Fraser Valley.

The game finally resumed. There was a grand slam. The crowd got into it. It was easily the most entertaining one we'd both seen in Korea. We would have missed it if we'd followed the rules.

A week later, Donna, the SAs and I went on a hike up Apsan, a mountain overlooking the city. It was a pleasant day. The path up wasn't very steep, or so I remember.

I lead the way. We saw the monument to the battle of Nakdong. I pointed out some Shilla era carvings and statues. We were never lost for a moment. Luckily, Serena and Bill brought Snickers bars and an orange.

They were pretty cultured folk. They were musical. They were hippies. They went to cherry blossom and butterfly festivals in towns I'd never heard of. Often they came back disappointed. Nature in Korea could be underwhelming.

I remember Bill saying, "There were thousands of butterflies alright – all pinned to boards in a packed expo hall."

We posed for a few pictures on a big rock overlooking the city. Everything was laid out the same as you see on Google Earth.

There didn't seem to be much order in the design. Everything seemed to spread in random directions. Almost directly below us was Woobang Tower. There was a golf course. I could make out one of the military bases. Everything else was square as if formed by a cookie cutter.

All around the city, hills hold in the pollution. In the spaces between the drab, monotonous architecture there was a yellow, gray haze. Palgonsan, the great mountain to the north of the city, was almost completely obscured by it. On clear days it was imposing, but those, I was told, are now fewer and fewer.

We made our way back down the mountain. We passed though a temple. It was a much steeper descent than any of us had anticipated.

As it turns out, yellow dust, or huang-sa, was just starting to roll in from China. It's been going on for centuries, but now it mixes with heavy industrial metals I don't want to know about. At one time the dust only came in the spring, but now it comes year round.

After a dust storm the residue sits everywhere on cars and windows like fine, yellow chalk. After it rains you see yellow trails leading to storm drains. The whole scene began to make me feel like it was time to start building an ark.

There wasn't much you could do. You had to close your windows. You didn't exercise outside. You could feel it in the air.

I started to feel sick in the mornings. I'd feel better later in the day. I still worked out inside the gym. After, I didn't feel so bad. It was like my body couldn't filter out the pollution properly.

At one time a lymph node under my arm began to swell. It freaked me out, but after a week or so it eventually went away. I wondered if it could be connected to the foul environment.

Despite the ominous skies we all got together in the park when we could. The park was usually packed with people on weekends. Still, it was a nice place to get together and pass the day.

Sometimes John made an appearance. He'd been living in seclusion saving money. He said he'd been in Korea too long. He knew it was time to leave. To save money, he had to become a shut-in.

Crystal was also leaving soon. She planned a trip to Vietnam and then Thailand before she made her way back to England.

After the park one night we had dinner at the SAs. Crystal, Mark and Donna all came. After dinner we sat down to play Asshole. Donna put on Radiohead's *In Rainbows*.

I saw into everyone, their sly smiles and devilish thoughts. Light danced through all the bottles and around the playing cards. Serena had it out for me. She seemed to have all the luck. She made me drink over and over. I didn't feel too into it, but I had no choice.

35

I landed in Shanghai on an overcast morning. I caught a cab from the airport into the city to a hostel I'd booked for a few days.

I'd always wanted to see China. I was curious about the people, the culture and the geography. I suppose I was also drawn to the unknown – that was probably the biggest attraction.

The ride into the city was exhilarating. All the humanity unfolding commanded my attention. The tall apartment buildings in the suburbs before the city were full of life, though some areas looked like a dirty gash on your knee – life bursting out of every door and window like blood through a cut.

The taxi crossed a bridge into the heart of the downtown. At the hostel I had a moment to collect my thoughts. I knew absolutely no Mandarin. I was careful not to stray too far into the shadows.

After sorting out everything at my hostel, I stepped outside and found a beer. For a while I let myself get lost wandering around. Then, I found Nanjing Road and made my way to the museum situated on the grounds of the old horse racetrack.

Outside the museum I met a fellow who looked exactly like Jack Black. I followed him and his lady friend a little ways and when they stopped I decided I had to find out. As it turns out he was German. He said people often confused him for the comedian.

He said they were just relaxing. They were in town for a little while. They said they had just come to Shanghai from Suzhou. I still had to make up my mind where to go during the week. I considered going there.

From the museum, I walked down the pedestrian section of Nanjing Road with my camera. I spent most of my time taking photographs, trying to get a sense of the mysterious city. I knew to be wary of thieves and anyone who wanted me to go with them to a teashop. People came up to me wanting me to buy their fake merchandise, but I wasn't in China to bring home junk.

Later, I took a cruise on the Huangpu River. I got to see the grand old buildings along the Bund and the imposing modern structures on the other side, in an area called Pudong. An unending line of boats, of varying size and shape, moved up and down the river. It was beyond explanation.

After I got off the ferry I saw a car hit a girl on a bike. Luckily, she seemed okay. Judging by the nonchalance that both parties reacted to the accident with, I assumed this type of thing happened quite frequently. No harm, no foul, I guess.

I wandered around the Bund as night approached. The whole scene was awash with vibrant color. I meandered a little while watching people slip in and out of the shadows. Then, I decided to let the night end.

I caught a taxi back to the hostel. I had dinner at a little place nearby with a couple of other travellers from the U.S. who had been in town a couple days. I was tired. I went to sleep listening to the strange sounds of midnight in Shanghai.

The next day I woke up early to visit Longhua temple, the oldest temple in the city. It looked to be quite a distance from the main tourist areas. Luckily, it was only a short subway ride from where I was staying. It was quite easy to find. Remarkably, it wasn't hard to find anything I was looking for while I was in Shanghai.

Inside the temple it seemed like every creature was enjoying the pleasant weather. Two young girls tried to toss coins through a tiny hole in a tall lantern. Some people stood quietly holding their hands together in prayer. Others lit sticks of fragrant incense leaving trails of smoke in the air. There were a few large cats lounging on wooden carts. In a quiet pond in the corner of the property turtles sunned themselves on rocks while white and red carp swam about.

The temple was first built during the Three Kingdoms period, an era that stretches from 184-280 AD. I first became acquainted with this period of time through my brother. When he was barely a teenager he used to play a 1st generation Nintendo game by KOEI called *Romance of the Three Kingdoms,* based on the story of the same name. I used to sit and watch him play the game.

According to a legend, Sun Quan, the famous King of Wu, obtained Sharira relics, or the cremated remains of the Buddha. To house these precious relics, he ordered the construction of 13 pagodas. Longhua Pagoda, part of the Longhua temple complex, is said to have been one of them.

The temple was destroyed by war towards the end of the Tang Dynasty and it was rebuilt in 977 AD, during the Northern Song Dynasty. The present architectural design follows the Song Dynasty original. The present Longhua Pagoda survives from that period, but most buildings in the temple were rebuilt during the Qing Dynasty. A modern restoration of the entire temple complex was carried out in 1954.

Extensive gardens and orchards originally surrounded the temple and monastery. Viewing of the peach blossoms in the Longhua gardens was an annual attraction for people in surrounding cities. These gardens have since been entirely absorbed into the neighboring Longhua Martyr's Cemetery.

From the cemetery I was able to take a picture of the pagoda rising above the garden, where all the trees and flowers were bursting with color. I was able to frame it so the urban sprawl growing around it was completely concealed. It left me with something to imagine how it had been.

Later that day I visited Yuyuan Garden, a traditional garden in the heart of the city. A bustling market surrounds it. People squeezed through the narrow streets lined with shops selling tea and souvenirs.

In the middle of all the shops I found the garden's entrance. I spent a few hours walking through the corridors looking at the fascinating architecture and design. It reminded me a lot of the Sun Yat-sen Garden in Vancouver.

Unfortunately, the garden was far too intricate to absorb all at once. I am sure I missed many significant features. I am sure every tree and rock held a story.

Afterward, along the street leading to the old French Concession area, I saw birds locked in cages in a miserable little park. Then, I passed a large crowd of people watching a lively game of mahjong. I took a few photos of all the action. After that I bought a few souvenirs for my brother and sister, wishing they were there with me.

36

I intended to go to Hangzhou or Nanjing for a few days, but the fellow who worked at the hostel told me it was easy to catch a bus to Huangshan. From there it wasn't hard to arrange transport to the revered mountain the city is named after. I thought it might be a stretch since I didn't have much time. However, he said that he was from Anhui province and that he could set up my accommodations.

Finding the bus station was the first real obstacle I faced. First, the taxi driver took me to the wrong place. There were all sorts of tiny bus companies operating. I went to each one to enquire. All I knew how to say was, "Huangshan." I went from one place to the next. I covered nearly the entire street. I was slowly loosing my patience and then it began to rain. Thankfully, an old man, sitting on a bench on the street I was pacing up and down, resolved my predicament.

He raised an open hand.

I said, "Huangshan?"

He nodded. He traced a path with his index finger. I followed it down the street, under the canal to our right and finally up to a large building about a five-minute walk away. I had to take a walkway under the canal to get to it. I bowed my head to thank him. He waved me away. Old folks can be a godsend.

It was a six-hour bus ride to Huangshan. I couldn't believe I was actually going to the great mountain.

Moving along the highway to somewhere I'd only seen in pictures was one of the most satisfying feelings I've ever had. Seeing this part of the world was an accomplishment long in the making.

Outside Hangzhou I noticed tea plantations high above on the steep mountainsides. Every now and then I could make out workers moving high above. The bus passed old villages with simple whitewashed houses. Deep gorges passed by in the blink of an eye. I tried to capture it all. It's all streaked in my mind now. It's been paired down to a few grainy images.

The bus exited the freeway, as it was growing dark. I thought my destination must be near. I listened carefully. The bus had gone hours without stopping, but now it was pulling over here and there to let people out. I wasn't sure where I was. In the dark, everything looked uninviting. The bus passed through dusty little villages where there were very few people. There were only a few lights in the distance.

It was completely dark when the bus made its final stop. The door opened, everyone exited and the bus pulled away. There wasn't any station - no maps, no information.

Everyone scattered. I didn't have a clue where I was or how to get where I needed to go.

I decided to take a rickshaw to my hotel. I showed the driver the address and a picture. I climbed in and the driver quickly had us moving. I was relieved. I sat back.

Not far from the station the driver pulled up to a restaurant. I tried to signal that this wasn't the place I wished to go. He insisted I go in. I decided to walk the rest of the way, thinking it couldn't be far.

I found what looked to be a main road. I could see all kinds of shops down narrow alleyways. Quite a few places had large piles of tea drying in front. It is impossible to describe the aroma.

The Anhui region is known for producing two of the most famous teas in China. They are Keemun, a rich black tea, and Mao Fung, an aromatic green tea. The mixture of so much tea drying in the air and in the shops was a delight I had not expected.

I kept walking. I turned down roads I had no business being on. I doubled back. I poked my head into shops. People eyed me with curiosity. Any mode of communication I had previously employed was utterly useless. Words weren't winning. My hand signals were entirely empty of meaning. I thought it might come to dancing.

I had a laugh at my situation. I just had to be patient. Everything was going to be okay. This was as bad as it was going to get. I tried to embrace the adventure.

During my walkabout, I noticed the entire sky had become a peculiar shade of purple, like the flesh of a blackberry. It was stunning. I stood for a second looking at the heavens and then they opened up on me. It poured rain, thunder cracked and lightning flashed close by.

The lights of the city flickered and then went out. All I had was the address for the hostel and a piece of map that showed the old part of the city.

Wiping water from my eyes, I decided I had to find a phone. I entered a shop and motioned to a young lady for help. I phoned the hotel, but they couldn't help me because I wasn't sure where I was.

I left the shop desperate to find a taxi. There weren't any that were empty, so I stood at a busy intersection, seething. Finally, I spotted a car with a beautiful bright light shining away - an empty cab. It pulled up and I looked in the window. It wasn't carrying anyone.

It turned out to be a friendly, English speaking police officer. He asked me how I was. He asked where I was from. He asked where I was going. Then, he drove me through the pitch-black city to my hostel about 10 minutes away.

I don't know if I would have found the place without his help. It was very foolish not to have specific instructions on how to get where I needed to go.

Tunxi, the area of Huangshan where I stayed, sits along the northern bank of the Xin'an River. There is a large stone gate at the entrance. The road is paved with massive stone slabs. It is lined with dozens of old shops that retain the ancient atmosphere. These buildings were built in styles that were popular during the Song, Ming and Qing dynasties.

The lights came back on as we arrived. People walking outside were just starting to put away their umbrellas. The many colored lights of the shops and restaurants, reflecting off the water on the ground, were mesmerizing. Faces flitted in and out of the shadows. Centuries seemed to pass with each blink. I was extremely relieved to be where I was supposed to be.

The hotel I stayed at was a pleasant surprise. It had been recently renovated. The staff was very friendly. As I checked in, a tiny puppy played at my feet.

After dropping off my gear, I sat drinking a Heineken on the veranda, laughing. I could see the famous stone gate. The bartender told me that across from us, literally twenty feet away, were two of the most famous restaurants in the region.

It was getting late. Outside there were still a few people. I was finally able to relax after the day's journey.

I went back inside and sat at the bar. It was quiet. The bartender said that there were only a few guests. They went to bed early so they would be well rested for the mountain. He told me he'd gone up it countless times as a guide. He said the next day wasn't going to be a great day to go. The forecast was for rain. Anyone who hiked up would be caught in thick fog. The steps would be wet and slippery and the going would be slow.

He told me there were two famous old villages just out of town. He said they were well worth a visit and that it would be much nicer weather down in the valley. I considered what he told me. I'd learned about the two cities when I was preparing lessons for the children's winter camp in January. I thought it would be a unique experience to see them. I still had one day to go up the mountain. I decided to take his advice. He told me he'd have the staff at the front arrange a bus tour for me. Perfect. I ordered another beer.

When I arrived, I was dripping wet. The hotel staff told me I could use their washer/drier. I put all my clothes in assuming they would be dry. Unfortunately, it only gave everything a little spin at the end. When I went back to check I found that every shirt I had was soaked. I went to bed worried that I would have to walk around in wet clothes. There wasn't anything I could do. I sat in bed flipping through Chinese TV, before nodding off.

At 7AM I walked outside in a slightly damp pair of shorts and a t-shirt. I carried a long sleeve shirt I hoped would dry so I wouldn't freeze. Thankfully it was humid and far warmer than I'd anticipated.

I sat in the street, in a corner of the square in the shadow of the old stone gate, waiting for my bus. The sun poked through the clouds. I watched as shopkeepers opened for the day. Many of the shops had large interlocking wood panels that had to be disassembled.

A light breeze picked up the fragrant scent of all the teas on offer. The quiet of the early morning slowly gave way to a low hum as more and more people opened up their shops. A few tourists began to buzz here and there looking at all the exquisite arts, crafts and teas of the region.

Finally, the bus to take me on my tour arrived. It was filled with ordinary Chinese folk taking a day tour. They all seemed to be wearing their Sunday best. I hadn't shaved. My hair was overgrown. My eyes were dark from lack of sleep. I tried to smile. It felt like the first day of school. I squeezed down the narrow aisle all the way to the back. Luckily, there was a seat by the window.

It was still early. The bus quickly made its way out of town. It crossed a bridge over a wide river. A construction crew had closed off one lane and traffic slowed. I imagined where the great mountain might be. The clouds were very low and I wondered if it would rain.

Traffic started moving again. The bus picked up speed. Before long the driver started on the horn. He swerved around all manner of vehicles. I saw an ox and farmer tilling a field flash by my view. The newness combined with the ferocious driving left me dumb.

Hongcun, the first city we came to, was where a few scenes from *Crouching Tiger, Hidden Dragon* were filmed. The preserved town was built in the shape of an ox. There was a pond in the center where people congregated. Ingeniously, drinkable water runs past each house from a river that passes from the west.

The old narrow streets were lined with young artists quietly working away and tourists moving in and out of old homes and shops.

Once again the scent of roasted tea filled the air. I sat down in the courtyard of a house with immense white walls, trying to drink it all in.

I spent much of my time there taking photos. There were so many unique images I felt rushed to capture everything. I wanted time to stop.

The morning was nearly perfect. The air was still and warm. The pond that fronts the town left a clear reflection of the green hills and unsettled sky. I envied the painters being able to spend time practicing their art.

After visiting Honcun we went to lunch. The two ladies who sat next to me were extremely courteous. They made a point to help me. They dished some food onto my plate. They poured some tea into my cup. Everyone seemed curious about how I would go about eating. Once they saw I could handle myself, it seemed a barrier was broken.

A few people could understand a little English and they asked me questions about who I was and what I was doing. An old man had one of the ladies ask me if I liked Chinese girls. For a while I was the center of attention. I got back on the bus feeling a little more at ease.

Xidi, although not as interesting as Hongcun, was also tremendous. It sits in a slight valley. Lush green hills rise in the distance. Like Hongcun there were groups of young artists on each street.

Once again, I ran around trying to take everything in. I wished I knew a little more about the history of each town. I bought a deck of playing cards with the names of all the famous buildings.

The people on the tour were very nice, though I don't recommend tours. The day dragged on as we were taken to a large silk shop and another large building housing local jewelry. I sat around while people did their shopping.

I thought the country would be a wonderful place to spend a year or two exploring. It was incredibly cheap and the people, from what I observed, were extremely friendly.

I got back to the hotel exhausted from all the exploration, but I had enough energy to walk across the street to enjoy some of the finest dining in the region.

Luckily, there were examples of each of the dishes the kitchen prepares in an area just outside the kitchen. To order I simply had to write the number of the dish I wanted and then hand it to a server. I was tempted to try some of the more exotic fare, but I didn't want to struggle up on the mountain with an angry stomach. I could've sat there all night trying the different specialties.

I went to bed excited. I was settled now for at least a day. I was getting used to some of the strangeness. As I settled into bed, I felt a surge of excitement. I would finally see the great mountain.

37

The road wound up the mountain much higher than I anticipated. The side of the road fell off steeply in some places. Only half way up the view was spectacular.

At the parking lot of the cable car station I bought a ticket to gain entry to the mountain and one for the ride up. I was surprised to see a long line of people already there.

Once again, the weather was cooperating. It was fresh and warm. The sky was clear. There was still a touch of moisture in the air, but I could tell it wouldn't last long.

I was disappointed I couldn't climb the trail to the top. The people at the hotel marked out the route I had to take if I wanted to make it back in time to catch a bus back to the city. The map was packed with information. I tried not to look at the places I wouldn't get to see.

Finally I reached the head of the line. I climbed in a car with a few others. I couldn't help staring at all that passed before me. I was completely mesmerized. Then, an old man shifted in his seat.

It was cooler at the top. I didn't mind because I anticipated having to move my ass. As I walked along the path I saw the natural shades of the alpine scene mixed with the colorful jackets of all the folks that had come for the hike. The mountain was packed with people taking in the majestic views.

At the top there were a few hotels where people stay so they can wake up and view the surroundings in the quiet of the early morning. I stopped at one to pick up a few supplies.

It was the beginning of spring on the mountain. There were plum blossoms. There were people of all ages. There were people you could hire to carry you up the steeper portions of the trail. All along there were workers carrying stones and supplies. They have calves like watermelons. They walk from the bottom with their loads.

All along the trails at the top I could see granite peaks emerging out of a sea of clouds. There are three peaks that rise over 1800 meters. The tallest is the Lotus Peak at 1864 meters. There are many different spots to look out from. There are many small delicate looking pine trees that hang precariously on the sheer rocks.

Li Bai, a famous poet from the Tang Period, came here. He is said to have named the mountain range. A teacher introduced me to his work in my first year of college. We read a poem called "The River-Captain's Wife – A Letter." I read a few others by him when I got the chance.

His poems use simple language, but they have a way of exploding in your mind. They somehow bring you closer to the divine. The mountain inspired him to write many famous poems. He compares the mountain to the lotus flower. The roots of a lotus begin in the mud, the stem grows up through the water, and the heavily scented flower lies pristinely above the water, basking in the sunlight.

I imagined the perspective he gained travelling here on foot, connected to the earth and how pristine it was, alone at the top with only the moon and food and drink you carried on your back.

In his travels Li Bai met many interesting characters. He writes about friends he met on solitary mountaintops. He writes about leaving them to journey down misty rivers. He liked to raise a glass with like-minded companions too.

Strangely, though he was an acclaimed poet, he lived a life of loneliness and hardship. He writes about this place as if it was his dear companion. Maybe it was all he needed. What more does a boundless imagination need than a clear view of the heavens and silence?

I don't know what it was like to spend time on the mountain the way the great poet did, but it's something I'd like to do if I ever get the chance. Unfortunately, now, hoards of people visit the mountain every year. It is a totally different scene.

I don't know what Li Bai might write about this world. I'd like to think he would be the same person. I am certain he would know a place to pick up good, strong wine.

On my short day tour I saw a great many stunning places, but I knew that there was so much more. In the distance, across a great gorge, I saw a walkway built on the sheer face of another peak. On it there was, what looked to be, a temple. I managed to find a few places where there weren't many people, but before I could settle I had to turn around and return to the main trail.

Before I knew it I was walking down. The steps were tricky. They were built for smaller feet, making it awkward to navigate. I had to go slowly and carefully. At the path to the Celestial Peak, the third highest on the range, I watched tiny brightly colored figures climbing up the narrow trail. I posed for pictures now and then with people I ran into. Near the end, there was colorful writing high on the sheer face of the mountain.

I met two brothers from Amsterdam at the bottom. They were the only other foreigners I saw that day. They said they walked up the day before, but didn't see a thing because of the heavy fog. They stayed the night in a hotel at the top. When they arrived they were told there weren't any beds. They said it was not the most pleasant experience, sleeping on the floor with thirty other men who wheezed and snored through the night.

They said they were up at first light. There weren't any showers, so they just went straight to hiking. They got to see a lot of the mountain, but one of them had a very sore foot. Coming down the mountain had been extremely painful.

We rode in the same bus back to Huangshan. One of the brothers worked in real estate and the other was a gardener. The gardener said he loved to see all the beautiful flowers that grew naturally in the hills. He laughed when he thought about how expensive some of them were back home.

They were heading back on a train that night and they had a little time, so I told them to join me at one of the restaurants across from where I was staying. We went to my hotel and I told them they could use the shower in my room. They were very thankful. It was nothing to me, but I could understand how they were feeling.

We went to the same restaurant I'd eaten at the day before. We arrived in the middle of the dinner rush. It was really hopping.

It was nice to share a meal and talk about some of the things we'd seen. They told me they had just finished a long bicycle trip through China. They started in the west. They peddled for two months. They said the weather was unholy. They had to jump in an airplane to get out of one area where there was flooding and mudslides and all sorts of misery. This was the final leg of their journey. They caught a train here from Shanghai. They would fly out in a couple days.

We talked about beer as we waited for our meal. They told me about drinking Suntory beer throughout China. They said it was the best stuff they'd found on their trip. I thought Suntory only made whiskey.

They asked me about Korean beer. I shook my head. There were no quality Korean beers that I knew of. I said the people didn't seem to demand better. Most didn't care as long as it was cheap.

Luckily there were a few import beers you could find at the convenience stores. Tsingtao made a good beer and I drank it often, but mostly I drank Heineken. Some friends drank Lowenbrau. And, there were a few American beers too, but nothing to write home about.

They wanted to know which would be the best direction to cycle across the U.S. They were thinking of doing that next. It made me think of doing something like that with my brother. Then I thought we'd probably kill each other. We've had some epic brawls.

The brothers were so thankful I let them use my shower they paid for dinner. I thought that was pretty considerate of them.

When they left I took a walk. I was tired from running around the mountain. I picked up some tea from one of the vendors and then returned to my room, exhausted and exhilarated.

I woke up the next day and caught the bus back to Shanghai. I was the first person on the bus this time. I sat right up front. The weather was unsettled most of the way. I knew I had to catch a plane the next day, so I was anxious everything would go smoothly.

As the bus neared Shanghai I tried to recognize something familiar from a few days before. The bus ended up pulling into an old, rundown station that was different than the one I left from two days earlier. I had no idea where I was, but the driver motioned to me to get out. It was the end of the line.

When I got off, I approached two policemen to see if they could point me in the right direction. I gave them my map and instantly a mob formed. Everyone at the station wanted to see what I handed over. I had to wade into the crowd to take back my map. There was nothing to do but walk until I found a taxi.

For a time, I was completely lost. Walking in the dry, dirty city was a definite contrast to the paradise I'd just visited. I tried to ask a few people that looked like they might be helpful - no luck. I tried to get some sense of where I was, but all I could see were unfriendly looking alleys and dusty dirty roads filled with traffic. It wasn't a scene you stopped to admire.

I peaked through some scaffolding that lined the street I was walking on. Through it I could see vast stretches of city that were completely razed; the flat, torn up ground went for miles. Beyond, there were weathered old buildings obscured by a smoky haze. They looked like rotting teeth.

Finally, I managed to flag down a cab. I hesitated at the door, trying to explain where I wanted to go and the driver took off with the door still open. I stood in a cloud of dust wondering what I'd done.

I stood for a while in the same spot unsure which direction I should take. It all seemed so hopeless.

After a few minutes another cab stopped. I didn't stand at the door this time. I got right in. I said, "Nanjing Dong Lu!"

The driver gave a nod. He smiled and said, "No problem."

He probably wondered how the hell I got so far off the tourist grid. I definitely experienced another side of the city.

He let me out on Nanjing Road across from Jing'an temple. I saw pictures of it on the Internet. I didn't think I would have a chance to see it. And there it was.

I took a second to look at the ancient architecture. It seemed entirely out of place next to all the modern steel behemoths that surround it.

I decided to make my way toward Pudong, the flashy new business district, on other side of the river. I thought it would be smart to find a clean, comfortable hotel that was close to the airport.

By the time I arrived there, it was dark and foggy. I knew there were lots of places to stay, but it was all far more spread out than I was expecting. Some of the buildings were unbelievably massive and I was dragging my ass around and glad I put in the time at the gym all winter.

After an hour of searching I found a room at the Novotel Shanghai Atlantis. The room was on the 43rd floor. It would have had a nice view of the Huangpu River if it weren't for the fog.

Before I left I had to get a massage. I booked one with the hotel and then went to find a place for dinner. As I was walking I grabbed a large bottle of Suntory beer. It tasted wonderful.

A little ways after, I came across a strange building. It had twelve massive Greek columns. It was lit up a searing white by spotlights and was decorated with exquisitely patterned gold leaf. There were expensive cars in the parking lot. All around, tall buildings rose up from the ground and out of sight.

I don't know what compelled me to go inside, but I am glad I did. It was an opulent spa, named the Shanghai Athens Basilica Star Bathhouse.

Inside, it looked like Caligula had a hand in the decor. It was the most luxurious place I'd ever visited. After some deft sign language I had a great Thai massage for a fraction of what it would have cost at the hotel.

After that I was done. I wanted to wander around a little that night, but I was utterly exhausted. I knew I would be sick in a week or so after I got back to Korea.

I walked back to my hotel as refreshed and relaxed as possible. I sank into sleep feeling the building's gentle sway.

I woke up early and took a taxi to the airport with almost no money to spare. I don't know why, but the taxi ride in the morning was much more expensive than the one I took into the city. As it turns out, the meal that the two brothers paid for was the difference between a peaceful exit and, what would have likely been, a scene. Thanks to them I got on my flight without incident.

A few weeks after my trip to China my school had a meeting with the staff from the other branches. I sat beside an English fellow I'd met a few times before. After the meeting wrapped, we decided to see a baseball game.

He was a nice guy, but he was still relatively new. He had been in Daegu for a few months. His school was closer to the center of Daegu. I thought he was having an easy time of it. He had a few of the usual gripes, but I didn't sense he had any major difficulties.

I told him I was starting to think about what I would do after completing my contract.

193

I liked the school I was at. It wasn't the best, but I had a lot of freedom to teach. I didn't have to worry about getting paid. I was leaning toward staying, but I also thought about going to Seoul, Taiwan, or even Japan. After going to China I was definitely more open to experiencing something different.

We watched the game. I imagined all my friends working away. I enjoyed a few beers. It was nice to have a mid-week break. It was an enjoyable diversion.

The next day at school, I found out the English fellow did a midnight run. He told his manager something happened with his family and left.

Yoon asked me about what we talked about at the baseball game. I told him I didn't know a thing. I was very surprised. I knew it looked bad.

He must have thought I was lying. Things around work soured just a little after that.

38

Donna and I arrived at the base of Palgonsan a little after noon. It was a near perfect day. There were a few clouds high above, but the majority of the sky was a rare deep blue.

We took the trail that starts just to the left of the entrance to the Donghwasa Temple. It was one of the most revered temples in this part of the country. It was founded in 493. It has a rich history too long to go into at length.

Long ago, it acted as a barrier for the Shilla Kingdom against invasion from the north. Now it housed one of the tallest Buddha statues in the entire world.

It wasn't intended to be a long hike. From the bottom you can see the sheer rock bluffs high above. I told Donna that we were going there. I don't know if she believed me. It wasn't that far on the map.

We made our way up slowly. We weren't in a hurry. It was delightful to finally be hiking up a mountain.

The path takes you through a forest of twisted pines. There were wild flowers here and there. It wasn't too hot. In the shade it was quite pleasant. On the trail up, Korean folks in hi-tech mountaineering gear smiled and waved.

Donna said she would be sad if I didn't come back. It was too quiet when good friends left. She faced the same problem I had in the winter: the only good people left were couples.

She told me Ben wasn't coming back. Earlier in the year visa regulations changed so that anyone with a criminal record was denied entry. He had some sort of petty misdemeanor on his record. I wasn't surprised. People like him would always run up against the law now and then.

She told me that while Ben was back in the U.S. he wrote the LSAT and scored very high. He considered law school, but he saw his future. He didn't see himself there quite yet. He was too young. She said he was going to teach in the Middle East or China.

I told her it felt as if I had seen everything I wanted to see in Korea. I liked Chilgok. I liked my job, but I wasn't satisfied. There was too much out there.

It wasn't long before we reached the top. Donna suggested we return the way that we came, but I didn't like that idea. I suggested we move east. She gave in. I have to admit I didn't quite know where I was leading us, but I never liked the idea of going back the same way if I didn't have to.

Along the top of the ridge we could see Donghwasa Temple and the tall standing Buddha. It looked like I could hold it in my hand.

The trail zigzagged, moving between forest and ridge. At one point, we made our way over large rocks that dropped off a great distance into the forest below. I could feel my heart beat pick up as I looked down.

After an hour I knew Donna was getting aggravated with me. She told me her ankle was really sore. She called me 'bossy.'

At the end of the trail we would arrive at Gatbawi, the famous stone hat Buddha sculpture. Unfortunately, we came to a spot where the path diverged. There was a trail down and I knew Donna had taken just about enough.

It was just as well. We walked in the cool shade alongside a clear babbling brook. In places there were clear pools of fresh mountain water that reminded me of lazy summer days at Cascade Falls in the back of my hometown.

The stream and the path wove alongside one another like a double helix. Now and then, beams of sunshine reached down through the forest illuminating her outline.

39

Before long Brian returned from Vancouver. He couldn't find anything in Daegu or Busan, so he lined up a half-decent gig in Ulsan.

He said he lived a little ways out of town by the airport. He had to catch a bus to work each day. He wasn't overly excited about the location, but the money was good. He sent a video of his new home to me recorded on his phone. It looked like just about everywhere else I'd seen.

He said he'd come up to Daegu soon and we'd get dinner at Joe's. It was something to forward to. A lot of times it felt like I was just counting down the days.

At the time a series of protests was happening in major cities throughout the country. They stemmed from the resumption of U.S. beef imports by the newly elected President Lee Myung-Bak.

Korea had a culture of protests. It's estimated that 11,000 protests happen each year. Some turned violent. This one went on for weeks. In Seoul, rioters set police buses on fire. A number of people were arrested. Earl told us about being caught in the middle of a riot while he was up there having his passport renewed.

Everyone in the country was talking 'Crazy Cow,' or Mad Cow Disease. It was on the cover of Maxim magazine. Kids I taught were absolutely sure they were going to go crazy if they ate beef from America.

In Daegu there were large vigils in the center of the town every weekend. One weekend, during an unrelated festival downtown I saw posters with a bull's skull and an American flag motif pasted all over the ground.

For a while I stayed away from the downtown. I didn't have much reason to go there already. When I did go to pick up supplies I didn't see anything untoward, but I wasn't feeling the love either.

The other teachers tried not to take the issue too seriously, but some of us felt there was some cause for concern when there were so many people in one area protesting something that was, from our perspective, so completely ridiculous.

Around this time, I was taking some cuts in the batting cage after work when the idea of a drinking game using the batting cage formed in my mind.

When Brian came up I told him about it while we sat outside a 7/11 drinking Heinekens. He said he was intrigued.

"Imagine trying something like it at home?" I said.

"We'll never get another chance," he answered.

"It might make other foreigners look bad – I mean, the terrible behavior."

"It would, wouldn't it?"

At Joe's the next week, I told everyone about Cageball. I laid out my vision. We refined the rules. Plans were settled over a number of bottles of soju. Obviously, Earl was on board. Donna didn't need convincing. Mark from England gave a quiet nod. The SA's thought it was fascinating. John was game. Brian and I would captain opposing teams.

I knew I was on to something. It was much more than a drinking game. By having teams there was an added element of competition. We were all fairly competitive people. The kicker was that anyone could do it. The balls didn't fly too fast. There would be lots of excitement. The trick was to get everybody locked in. They had to agree to drink.

The game was pretty straightforward. Before batting you'd drink a shot of tequila. The next time up you'd shotgun a beer. After that, you'd alternate between the two. Each time you stepped into the cage you would be drunker.

There were clear standards. You needed to hit the ball. The ball had to reach beyond the wall behind the pitching machine for 3 points. It had to get out of the batting box for one. A strike and a ball were worth 0 points. There were 15 balls per at bat. A perfect score was 45

The way the game was laid out none of us would remember afterwards so keeping track of the score was essential. The player on the opposing team next to bat would keep track. It was clean and simple.

On a warm Saturday night in late May we assembled the tequila and beer and then gathered at the batting cage in the center of town. We did a ceremonial round of tequila shots.

After five innings we called the game. We were all heavily inebriated. I don't believe anyone was injured, but it was starting to become unsafe. Brian's team won, but all of us were winners. Earl, the smooth swinging Texan was the obvious MVP. His 24 points in one at bat was the benchmark, though everyone put up decent numbers.

Somehow we all ate galbi after the match, but that memory is a wash of colors and blurry faces. It clouds over completely after that.

The next day we all got together to talk about what happened. John, the biggest fellow, and perhaps the most seasoned drinker out of all of us, told us the story that earned him the Most Sportsmanlike award.

Along with alternating shots of tequila and shot-gunning cans of beer, he finished a 60 of Jack Daniels. After dinner he got on his bicycle to go home, but the next thing he was conscious of was an old man leaning over him to see if he was okay.

It was light out. He was lying in the grass just off the sidewalk. He was still on his bike. He somehow toppled over and stayed out cold for hours. While he told us the story he showed us the grease on his leg from where it rested on the chain. None of us could remember ever seeing a foreigner out cold on the street. Cageball brought him to the edge.

Everyone decided we had to play one more time to see if we could finish an entire game.

40

About this time Brian's brother, Colin, also came back to Korea. They were staying together in Ulsan until he could find work. A few of us decided to meet the brothers in Busan to celebrate Buddha's birthday.

For the trip down I prepared a concoction of fruit - lemons, strawberries, mangos and oranges – and vodka. I put it all through a blender and stored it in my freezer over night.

At around 1PM we got a hotel room off the main strip in Haeundae. It was big enough to fit all eight of us. We relaxed a little while waiting for Brian and Colin, but they phoned and said they were held up and wouldn't make it until later.

I was pretty familiar with Busan. I could find a few key places. I took everyone to a little Mexican restaurant tucked down a narrow alley near Haeundae before we set of to visit the temple.

To get there, we caught a bus to the east end of the city. It took us away from the beach and around a steep hill before returning to the coast. I thought it must be the same route I took on my first trip to Busan.

At the end of the line there was a little strip of restaurants and hotels that overlook another beach. From there, the temple was just a short taxi ride away.

Before going to the temple everyone needed to resupply. While we waited we posed for photos with a large group of university students who were also enjoying the holiday. By this time I'd long since finished the jungle juice. I was pretty well ready for anything.

Haedong Temple sits right on the coast overlooking the sea. For Buddha's birthday the temple had arranged hundreds of colorful lanterns.

The sun began to set as we explored the temple grounds. The sound of waves crashing below, along with the aroma of incense and salt mixing in the howling wind, made it one of the most awe-inspiring places I visited in Korea.

Before long we'd all seen enough. We'd run out of fuel and the wind was surprisingly cool. We made our way up the slight hill to the main road where were hailed a couple taxis.

We met Brian and Colin on the boardwalk that runs along Haeundae beach. It was good to see them together again. Together they are like three people. The night was immediately transformed.

After a quiet dinner we went to the U2 bar for a nightcap. Most of the rest of the night is a blur.

In the morning, Colin was nowhere to be found. He wouldn't answers his phone, so Brian started to get really concerned. He said Colin could be unpredictable. He had a reputation for nocturnal wandering that sometimes got him into trouble.

We eventually found him sitting on the beach smoking a cigarette. By that time the sun was high up there nice and high. Morning was the only calm time in Korea. I didn't ask him what happened.

After lunch, most of us caught a bus across town to see a lighthouse on the cliffs in the southwest corner of the city. Donna and the SAs stayed behind to lie on the beach. I told them they were missing out.

It was a long bus ride, as it turns out. Colin told us he wasn't going to be allowed to teach in Korea again. Immigration had permanently labeled him an 'unsavory character.' He said it was probably due to an incident that occurred in Montreal at the Korean consulate.

He nearly started a fight on the packed bus when a young fellow gave him a push as he passed by. I calmed him by opening a one liter can of Sapporo beer a random Korean fellow bought for Donna after the bar the night before.

We reached Busan Station and got out to take a breather. We threw a Frisbee in a parking lot while we waited for another bus. I finally found a place to buy one the day before. I was pretty satisfied with myself until I tried to bounce it off the pavement and it shattered.

After that, and the purchase of a bottle of cheap gin, we boarded another bus to get to our destination south of the city.

The bus weaved around the rocky coast. The machinery of the port obscured most of the scenery. It was all bright metallic reds, blues and yellows. Further from the city there were more tall white buildings built up along the coastline. There were more bridges in the distance than I cared to count.

We told Colin about Cageball. He wanted in. We set up another game for the summer solstice.

We walked up the path to the lighthouse. The wind whistled in the thick forest of pines. When we reached the cliff, there was a rosy pink sky above the dark blue sea.

The lighthouse was built high above the shore. There was a stairway from it, down to another section where you could walk around and get a different view. There weren't too many people. I watched ships moving here and there. We were all pretty spent at that point.

A few weeks later, Donna, Mark from England, The SA's, the Texans and I went to Pohang to try to catch a fish. Again, we would meet the brothers there.

Often at Thursday dinners Earl and I ended up talking about fishing. I told him about Saskatchewan. He said that before he arrived he'd spent time spear fishing in the Dry Tortugas. He told me about an encounter he had with a mako shark. We didn't expect a lot from Pohang, but we both looked forward to trying our luck.

We spent the night before the trip getting stonecold drunk at Joe's. We didn't have to work on Friday so it was an extra special. It was getting warmer. We all celebrated and posed for photos. At the end of the night there were tables littered with bottles of beer and soju and plates of food that Joe kept bringing from the kitchen.

The train ride to Pohang was short and peaceful. I watched the scenery pass. In the valley, rice grew tall and green. Earl sat beside Sue, scribbling in his book of adventures. The SAs were mildly exuberant. Mark from England slept in the seat in front of me. Donna sat beside me, serenely. We were all pretty excited to find a place to charter a boat and get out on the water.

When we arrived we found Brian sitting on the steps outside the station. He was smoking a cigarette and talking on his phone. Next to him was a large bottle of Cass Red.

The scene outside the station wasn't promising. It was searing, dry and dusty. I couldn't see anything natural other than a few old folks sitting under the shade of a crooked pine tree a few steps outside the station. I couldn't help noticing an impeccably dressed old man in a black three-piece suit. He wore a fedora that matched. He sat there so calm. I was wearing a t-shirt, baking in the heat.

Brian told us that Colin couldn't make it. He had to stay behind to have an interview over the phone with a company in Japan. It looked like he was going there.

We all took photos as we walked through a market between the train station and the sea. There was a badly burned nightclub outside a convenience store. All around the market there were tiny silver fish drying on racks. We accosted merchants and townspeople and some posed for pictures with us.

We could have tried to get to someplace a little more attractive. We could have hopped right back on the train. Pohang certainly wasn't winning any beauty contests, but the next stop would likely be more of the endless sameness.

One glimpse of the sea made me realize it was no place for fishing. Crossing a bridge, I took an ice cold, yellow chicken foot that Donna purchased at the market and dropped it into the ocean. It slowly disappeared into the thick, chalky water.

At Songdo beach, Earl and Brian managed to find some locals who knew where we could find a boat. They gave us directions to a tiny dock down from where we were. We found it at the mouth of the river that cuts through the town, across from the giant Posco Steel plant.

Earl sorted everything out at the dock. I thought there was no way anyone would take us on the water, but before I knew it we were gathering our gear onto the boat. Before we left the shore, Donna showed a couple local boys how to shotgun a beer.

We didn't get too far before the captain dropped anchor. He set us right next to some giant concrete breakwaters. Bill told us a South African invented them. Old men sat up on them while they fished. Sea gulls flew high in the blue sky.

I couldn't concentrate much on fishing, especially when I saw the meager tackle the captain provided us with. There was only one rod. The captain tied on a piece with a series of tiny hooks. He indicated to us that we needed to put on some tiny shrimp for bait.

I threw out one cast. After that I handed the rod to Earl. He was livid. I wanted to tell him to calm down. Brian came to the back of the boat, saw what we were doing and gave his head a shake. It was all pretty pitiful.

Either way, I couldn't think of eating seafood. After a while I found a spot on the bow with everyone else. There was nothing to do except enjoy the sun's rays and the boat's gentle sway.

The captain must have had a good laugh, considering how much he charged us. I don't think we were on the water more than an hour before he decided to pull up anchor. We *did* manage to get out on the water.

Returning to shore, the sun was blanketed by high cloud, leaving a sort of rusty haze. In the distance, north of the train station, there were tall white apartments rising all along the coast. Just as in Chilgok, these apartments were home to young families. They were, what amounts to, the middle class – doctors, dentists, engineers, lawyers, teachers and housewives - all those round people in their square holes.

They all depended on one thing, Posco. It was one of the largest steel companies in the world. Since opening it has produced enough steel for 250 million cars. The massive corporation gets its steel from all over the globe. It planned to build a plant in India. On paper it makes sense to move someplace where labor costs are less expensive. For a while Korean specialists and engineers will go there. However, the laborers will be Indian, or from someplace poorer.

I wondered what the future might bring. I saw the gargantuan factory decaying back into the earth. I saw all the waste seeping into creeks, on into rivers and, finally, into the sea. I didn't see anyone coming to the rescue. Maybe somehow they'd turn it around. Maybe they'd turn it into an amusement park.

When we got of the boat I noticed a solitary windsurfer coasting along. Maybe I was looking at everything all wrong?

Before long it was night. We wandered a little, before deciding to go to a wholesome American franchise family restaurant. It was loud. It was tacky. It offered something for everyone.

We ordered a team pitcher. I remember laughing so hard at one point I was crying - I hadn't laughed that long and hard since I was in teenager, skipping school and up to no good.

It was all in good fun. Sue lost a newly purchased hat and was in a panic. Earl, who sat next to her, was wearing it. He had a fantastic look of concern on his face. He kept telling everyone to give it up. He looked so serious. It went on for about ten minutes until he put it back on her head. I didn't know if she was drunk or dumb. I told our waitress it was Brian's birthday and she returned with a few others to sing,

205

"Happy Birthday." Brian sat cockeyed through the ordeal while the rest of us had another laugh.

After, we ordered cocktails like we'd really been out to sea - it wasn't long before a manager came over and told us to leave. Outside, we stood around taking in the nightlife. The main drag was a narrow strip with a curious stream running down the middle. We gathered around a square built like a wrestling ring. Its surface was lit up. I wondered what it would look like if two people got up on it and started to wrestle. It would make a great show seeing two people scrapping as people streamed by.

There was no night culture to speak of in Pohang. There were just places to get drunk. We ended up in a foreigner bar with a decent pool table. The bar had Jagermeister and Red Bull. It had cheese puffs. We made a good time of it.

At around 3AM a few U.S. Special Forces walked in. They seemed like decent people. One fellow said he was studying for a Master's degree in chemistry. Another requested the music be changed to something thuggish. About then we decided it was time to call it a night.

When I woke up I wasn't sure where I was. The jagerbombs had done a number. The room looked a little worked over, like someone had been searching frantically for something. I gathered my things, took a sideways look in the mirror and slipped out.

I recognized the street from the night before. I remembered talking to the marines and cheese puffs flying through the air. I remembered throwing a half full tallboy as far as I could down a street. There were a lot of gaps, a lot of black.

I met Donna and the South Africans at the neon square. They weren't feeling well either. They couldn't fill in much of the story, though Donna said I was responsible for the room.

I called Brian a few times, but he wasn't answering. We walked toward the station. The four of us had had our share of Pohang.

We sat at the station a little while waiting for a train or a phone call. We were minding our business when a raving fellow with what looked to be dried ketchup on his upper lip stood in front of us, mumbling and fidgeting. He made the SA's uncomfortable.

An old lady looking on said something to the man and he lumbered off. I shook my head and laughed. She offered us dried minnows and soju. How could I turn her down?

The train ride back was fabulous. We still had two more days off. After seeing Pohang, it was nice to return to the relative peace and quiet of the Gok.

A few days later I ran into Earl. He told me that he stayed with Brian in Pohang another night. They each bought a fishing rod and tried casting from shore. While they were there a fellow came up to them with a fish he'd just caught and gave them some raw flesh.

I thought about what I would do next. I still didn't have a clear picture of where I'd be, but I enjoyed teaching. I told the kids at school I wasn't going to be coming back.

They taught me a great deal. Some challenged my mind. Some challenged my patience. Some were open; they talked to me and asked questions. Others didn't want to take part. You can't force them to learn.

I decided to make the last few classes as fun as possible. I knew the younger kids would immediately take advantage, so I didn't change their lessons. I played a little Jack Johnson or Pearl Jam for the well-behaved middle schoolers, while they wrote their essays for presentation class.

I taught a lot of the same children for the entire year. I wondered if I'd see any of them again. I hoped I would.

41

A week before my birthday John came back from Seoul with Cageball jerseys. We each had our nicknames sewn on the back. Ben called me D-War, after the dreadful Korean Movie. It stuck. There was also, Lowball, The Colonel, Juiced, Dropout, The Ringer, Dangerous, and Cosa Nostra.

We played our final game on the summer solstice. It was also my birthday. A year earlier I was fishing in Saskatchewan. I wasn't sure I would remember this one.

Colin and Brian came to Chilgok from Ulsan the day before. We stayed up drinking long into the morning. It was light out when we ran into Joe. He was walking down the street toward us, on his way home after closing his restaurant.

He joined us at another BBQ restaurant for some meat and drink. It was the first time I saw him out of his restaurant. We showed him the logo on our jersey incorporating his restaurant's name, a baseball and a Roman numeral three set in front of green mountains. He had a big smile. He was so appreciative of our patronage throughout the year he paid for everything.

The next day the game went ahead. We quickly took care of all the administration. We had a tub filled with ice and around fifty cans of beer. There were two bottles of cheap tequila. John brought another big bottle of Jack Daniels.

The atmosphere during this game was far more intense than I ever could have anticipated. Everyone brought a camera. We had as close to total coverage as could reasonably be achieved. I've never seen so many people focused on a single stall at a batting cage.

We worked the system of scorekeeping to perfection. Actually, it revealed a great deal about the event. The numbers started out orderly and for the first few innings they stayed that way. Around the third inning the writing began to unravel. It became less legible the further the game went on.

This time we managed to make it to the seventh inning. I am not sure what happened after that. I am told I was found in my apartment pacing around naked, speaking in fragments.

When I awoke I saw Colin and Brian in my spare room. Donna was beside me, snoring. We had a pleasant enough morning considering the carnage.

As it turned out, my team won. Brian and Sue were both injured. Bill took home MVP. He used a cricket swing that was surprisingly effective.

Earl was the most sportsmanlike. During one of the final at bats, a ball struck Brian's thumb. He dropped to the ground, writhing in agony. Instantly, Earl stepped into the cage, over his fallen teammate, to pick up the bat. He bunted a few balls for points, while a few others checked on Brian. It was, I can say quite confidently, the most poignant moment in the history of the game.

We went down to Mule's new place, called The Pork Pit, the day after the match. He asked me if I was going to stay on another year. I told him I didn't see it happening. He apologized for hockey never materializing.

After lunch we took a walk to the temple in the middle of town that I'd visited in the winter. We made our way up to the cathedral on the hill. I showed everyone the hand of god.

We made our way through the city toward Dalseong Park. At the zoo we saw poor animals in cages looking pitiful in the oppressive heat. There were lions, tigers and bears – each and every one locked down for our viewing pleasure.

You didn't see too many wild animals in Korea. It was strange to see even one. You almost didn't want to. Odds are it'd be a sketchy, post-traumatic alley cat.

We stood at a railing looking over at a savagely undernourished tiger. Earl said, "When you see an animal like this, you can't help but want to throw something at it - get it fired up. You hope it'll get mad and find the will to escape. And then you hope it'll understand you were doing it a favor."

"It's not right."

"It's fucked up."

"Anyone got a coin?"

Sometime later Brian and I played our last game of pool. It was the same night as Roger Federer and Raphael Nadal's Wimbledon epic. There were a number of rain delays in London. We played on while waiting to see what would happen on the other side of the globe.

Both of us played over our heads. I made one or two shots I'll never likely make again. I remember distinctly one jump shot that cleared nearly the whole table before cutting a ball sharply into the corner. We were both stunned for a few seconds. Brian made some incredible bank shots. He also overcame his tendency to miss the longer ones.

At about 3AM the tennis match resumed. The place had long been empty. The fellow supervising the pool hall let us keep playing. He communicated that he didn't mind. He was watching the tennis too. He bought us a few beers from down below, when he went to get a pack of cigarettes.

Time passed. We drank. We played more pool. The more you play the better you should become. Unfortunately, it doesn't work out that way. For me it is a failure to live in the moment, the time when everything matters. We each hit a few more shots that were out of this world. After a while they were almost expected.

Sitting down between games I tried to capture the scene. Lights buzzed in the empty hall. Outside the city lights were still strong.

"It never flickers. It's always full throttle here. What if one day it all stops?"

"I wouldn't want to be here then either," answered Brian.

"How's your brother?" I asked.

"He's loving Japan. He's forgotten this place."

Every once in a while we leaned over and saw something spectacular on the TV screen.

"People will forget this tennis match too." I said.

"It'll slip away."

"A footnote," I added.

"Not even."

"I can't wait to get the hell out of here."

At that point I still didn't know what I'd do. I couldn't go back to what I did before coming to Korea. I didn't seem to fit anywhere anymore. I knew it was likely I would end up back in this part of the world before too long.

Either way, I was getting back on a plane soon. Home. Lotusland. I told Brian about the welcome my sister planned for me – a big bag of Kush.

I told him about the golf course I would play, a little ways outside Vancouver on the north bank of the Harrison River.

Brian said, "I can't wait to smoke again."

"Before long I'll be taking a long walk in the enchanted forest."

"And I'll still be here in the bad bush."

It crossed my mind that I might come back someday. Seoul was an option, but I heard that you're expected to really work there.

The game came back on after another delay. It seemed like each point was greater than the last. The three of us were spellbound.

During a break, the man told us his daughter went to a nearby English academy. Neither of us had heard of it. There were so many English academies it was impossible to keep track of them all. He proudly showed us a picture of her he had saved on his phone. She looked exactly like a student I taught earlier in the year.

The rain stopped the match once more and we decided to call it a night. We said goodbye. We thanked him for letting us stay so long. We made our way out down the stairs. Out in the street there was still a touch of neon, but past it, just over Hamjisan, there was a single brilliant shining star just beyond the sinking sky.

3124908R00129

Printed in Germany
by Amazon Distribution
GmbH, Leipzig